STONES
AND
SWITCHES

D1518348

STONES AND SWITCHES

Lorne Joseph Simon

Theytus Books Ltd.
Penticton, British Columbia

Copyright © 1994 Lorne Simon

THEYTUS BOOKS LTD.
257 Brunswick St., Penticton, B.C., V2A 5P9

Book Design and Typesetting: Marlena Dolan
Cover Art: Roger Simon
Back Cover Art: Teresa Marshall
Cover Design: Richard Gray

Printed and Bound in Canada

Canadian Cataloguing in Publication Data

Simon, Lorne Joseph, 1960-1994
Stones and Switches

ISBN 0-919441-68-8

I. Title.
PS8587.I35S76 1994   C813'.54   C94-910648-8
PR9199.3.S55S76 1994

The publisher acknowledges the support of the
Canada Council, Department of Communications
and the Cultural Services Branch of the
Province of British Columbia in the publication of this book.

A part of Chapter 9, the story that Mr. Severman reads, previously appeared in a slightly different form in *Gatherings: The En'owkin Jour-
nal of First North American Peoples, Volume III*, published by Theytus
Books, under the title *Webs*.

THANKS

First of all, to my parents, Sarah and William John Simon Sr., for all the stories; to En'owkin, and their great staff, for nurturing talent; to Maurice Kenny, for the '92 writer's retreat where I wrote the first chapter; to my brothers, Adam and Jesse, for letting me have their place for the summer of '93, when I wrote the rest of the book; to Richard Van Camp, for his enthusiasm and critiquing; to George Haley and Lynda Doige for their helpful comments to parts of the story; and, finally, to Gerry William and Jeannette Armstrong for their invaluable suggestions. Hey, and thanks, Sher, for everything.

With love to my mother,
Sarah,
who told me the story –
and knows better than I do
what really happened to Megwadesk.

CONTENTS

Chapter One

Caught In An Invisible Net

Six days had passed since he chose this location. Six accursed days. He had set his three-and-a-half inch gillnet where the shallows once jostled with fleeing minnows and feeding striped bass. The young man stared at the floats of his net. The floats bobbed too lightly; the lazy wavelets easily rocked them. Disgustedly, he threw a pair of dice into the shallows. They plunged and spouts leapt like brief flames in their wake. Then the dice reemerged; around them two rings formed and increased. Their ripples collided into each other.

Megwadesk sensed that it would be another eerie night, filled with intimations of evil. He bit his thumbnail and pulled it with his teeth. He hissed as he tore off some skin but the pain roused him.

For a minute, the northern corner of the sky was a ghostly white cobweb. Then darkness, in ever-thickening swarms, advanced. The last dull threads of light drooped over the raspberry bushes and on the scattered stunted fir, creating a jagged silhouette looming over the young man. The wavelets crouched along the shore and sighed. They split the pale moon's reflection repeatedly but the moon always emerged whole behind the gleaming crests.

The sun had set but the heat persisted. Megwadesk yawned and brushed the flies from his face. Sweat glued his shirt to his narrow back. Both shirt sleeves were wet from wiping his brow.

Megwadesk Ligasudi. That was his name. Megwadesk meant, "Red-flashes-striking-into-the-sky." Megwadesk was one of the Micmac names for the northern lights. The

Micmacs believed that red northern lights prophesied war. Megwadesk was born in the Moon of Fattening Animals – Wigewigús, October – and the northern lights had shaken and veiled and slithered red across the sky. Now his head ached and in his mind flashed anger.

I'm hexed! he thought. *That's all there is to it, eh. I'm bewitched! Meda, what else's gonna explain this, eh? No more than thirty yards from my net is Skoltch's net. Nisgam, might just as well say we're staked 'longside each other, eh! Still I don't never catch a thing 'tall! But he - well, every morning I see'm! Yes siree, I do! He rows out in his ugly, green boat, to check his net. Up 'n' down he goes, eh, an' he's flinging 'board bass as long as my arm! Right 'n' left he's chucking 'em in, like crazy! Well, geez, it's almost like this river's his own hatchery, his dam 'n' his dam only! Nisgam nuduid, he's hauling in hundreds of pounds 'n' me - well, geez, not even a lousy minnow 'tall, eh! Now that he catches so much 'n' I get nothing in this same spot, nothing 'tall – well, that can't be nothing else but witchery! Éhe. I know the channel here. My net's set in a good place, eh. Right here it was, yep, that I saw the water roil with bass. Right here! Now he's taking it all. Nisgam, it's crazy!*

There were dark pillows under his reddened eyes. For the past six nights he had slept very little and, of the little sleep he got, none of it had been restful. A dreadful web seemed to surround him, visible only to his shut eyes. Always his spirit's nightly flights ended in a tangle of nightmares. Something always chased him in his dreams. He got no satisfaction from sleep, no rest. So now he avoided sleep.

He tried to stay busy to keep his blood running. During the days he cleared a road near the top of the hill to make the new house, that he was building for Mimi and himself, accessible to horse-drawn wagons. All day, every day, he chopped trees to make a road until the skin on his palms was thick and deeply wrinkled as the bark of an old oak. At night he watched his net.

Now, to stay awake, Megwadesk kept turning his neck and looking around, trying to keep his heavy eyes from crossing. For the past forty-eight hours he had not so much as taken a nap. He unsheathed the knife strapped to his belt. He picked up a piece of alder and absently whittled on it.

Low clouds drifted in. The clouds glowed as they ap-

6

proached the moon and turned murky as they slipped under her and hid her. Night smothered the amber cinders of twilight. Megwadesk felt the air currents alternating. The occasional touch of cool breeze felt good.

Yes, he thought, *a storm's blowing over this way.*

The breeze gradually softened until the only air moving was breath. Half the sky still glittered with stars and the river opened into another glowing sky and the farther shore seemed magnified, brought closer by the doubling of its image. Perfectly reproduced inverted white pines appeared to nest several motionless teals and a pair of loons.

Megwadesk thought about legends of two-horned serpents living under water in lodges and in a country every bit like the one on the surface. *Did them old storytellers,* he wondered, *dream up a World-Below-the-Water from looking at reflections, eh? Then's that world to be pictured as upsidedown?* He wondered if he was thinking like this only because his world now seemed overturned.

On the water the cackling of mallards was immediate, as though they were not by the other bank but in the reeds near the net. The springwater spouting from the sandstone across the river gurgled, it seemed, just off to his right. Every sound was as close as the hiss, hiss, hiss of his blade slicing into alder to send chips flying. The grey owl in the forest sounded like she was nesting on Megwadesk's nape, hoo-hooing, hoo-hooing, and then retiring into a breathing as intimate as the purring of a house cat.

"Chigdeg," Megwadesk murmured the Micmac word for such profound stillness. The leaves of the birch and the fluffs of sea-fowl down caught on the grasses by the river were motionless.

He remembered spearing eels on a night similar to this one.

It had been over a month ago. The river was placid then. A hand-size trout breaking the water would have made one swear that an Atlantic salmon had splashed. Alone on the boat, Megwadesk had drifted for hours, standing on the deck, peering into the underwater shadows cast by the lamplight, striking at the occasional eel and tossing it aboard.

Suddenly someone whispered into his left ear, "Are you having much luck?"

Startled, Megwadesk wheeled around but there was no one there. He thought how sometimes a man imagined things when he was alone on the boat for too long.

"Here I am," the voice said again and Megwadesk spun to his right.

Nobody. Then the voice added, "On the shore, below the poplar ridge."

And there on the shore, almost a half-mile away, stood a man in white. His voice had carried over the buffed-chrome surface of water as though through an invisible tunnel, so that even the subtlest nuances came as crisply as consonants to the fisherman's ears. The rich acoustic quality of the river on such a still night had surprised Megwadesk. He had only to answer evenly for the man in white to hear him.

"I got nothing 'tall. Maybe just a dozen," he said.

The man in white on the far shore then raised his arms and answered, "Come over to this side of the river, my brother. You will find eels streaming over the shallows. So numerous are they, my brother, that you would mistake them for clusters of seaweeds swaying in the tide."

Megwadesk poled across the river. He watched the man in white turn and climb the hill above the embankment until he merged into the towering gloom of poplars. And, indeed, there had been eels near where the man in white stood.

What impressed Megwadesk was how effortlessly sound carried on such rare nights. Air, he realized, could change distance the same way water did. When spearing eels, a man never struck the eel's image that the water sent up, for that was a trick of nature. A man judged the depth of the water and then struck short of the image according to this estimate. Megwadesk realized a similar trick of nature, where distance seemed to change, happened through sound on certain nights. And that made him wonder how many spirit stories originated from nature's tricks. After all, he had been about to row home and tell his spouse, Mimi, that a ghost whispered in his ears while he was spearing eels. Had he not finally spotted the man in white on the shore, he would have never realized it was the combination of unusual stillness and near perfect acoustics that had lent the man's voice such eerie travelling power. That was over a month ago.

Now Megwadesk peered thirty yards to his right at the

net belonging to Skoltch. He expected a tremor to vibrate the surface line any second. He momentarily expected rows of wavelets to emanate from Skoltch's net. Night after night he had stood in vigil and had seen this happen while his net remained dead. How he longed for ripples to shudder from his net instead! Only a bass thrashing on his net would assure him of his skills.

Either my luck changes shortly, eh, or I find 'nother trade, he thought. *Or I soon do something drastic.*

He pressed his palm against an open blister at the base of his thumb. Again the pain revived him.

I've never stolen in my life, Megwadesk thought. *Not 'tall, but now's that something to be proud 'bout, eh? Maybe I just never had to steal. Maybe I was never tempted, eh. Can I be proud 'bout being so straight when I never had to fight temptation?*

Faith in himself used to rest on moral excellence. But now Megwadesk scoffed at that notion and he wished he could steal to prove that he could do something – even something wrong – out of sheer strength of character.

Across the river Megwadesk saw two dark shapes, one larger than the other, steal down a trail to reach the spring gushing from the sandstone riverbank. It was a doe and her first yearling. He did not feel so drowsy any more. The presence of large game excited him.

He remembered a hunting story that his cousin, Talon, once told him, a story about how Talon had killed a buck three years ago. Talon had dreamt he was wrapped in fire. Because he was unharmed, he knew he was being cleansed for something. Then the fire vanished and Talon was standing beside a familiar brook and it was dawn. In his dream Talon watched as several deer appeared from the woods to drink. Talon told Megwadesk that it was still dark when he had woken.

"I was sure if I left right away to get to the creek I had dreamt about – well, I was sure if I left just right then that I would find deer there!" he had told Megwadesk. "I had this feeling, like I could make my dream real, like I could pull it into this world, aye! Éq, that's exactly how it felt!"

Talon told Megwadesk how he had taken his 30-30 rifle and his hunting knife and ran four miles through the night to the place he dreamt about. All along, he told Megwadesk, it seemed like he was racing through a dream. The wind in his ears sounded like the cleansing fire in his dream. The air had been thick with dew. When he reached the brook, there were no deer.

"I crouched perfectly still for about ten minutes," Talon told him. "Then light began to glow in the east. Nisgam, I can't describe how excited I was, aye! My insides tingled. And then it was like I was reliving something exactly as I had seen it years and years ago! The deer appeared! Nidab! I looked and there were deer! Deer! Just like in my dream! Gisúlk, my stomach felt like it was being ripped! Nidab! That's what I say – fate was gutting me! It wasn't until I shot the deer that I broke the spell. I was all soaked in sweat. I was sick to my stomach. I hardly had enough strength left to slit the deer's throat and bleed it. I lay down on the bank for a long time, dead with fear. Finally I got up and made a small fire, threw cedar in it, burned berries for the deer and then rested. Éq, nidab, again I lay back and rested. After a while I was just filled with happiness! Éq, a feeling of greatness returned my strength like I'd just discovered a new set of muscles in me, invisible muscles I'd never before used in my life! Nisgam nuduid, I felt like leaping around! My feet were filled with power! I gutted the deer and carried it home on my back."

Megwadesk remembered that just three weeks ago, when Talon asked to borrow an eel-spear from him, Talon had said, with a fanatical blaze in his eyes, "Eels are waiting for me at the breakwaters. "The certainty in Talon's eyes had convinced Megwadesk. Megwadesk knew that it was intuition that separated a mere skilful fisherman from a proficient fisherman and a strong hunch expressed itself with conviction. Besides, Megwadesk had been doing well with his net then and he believed that his luck returned to stay for the summer, so he had let Talon have the spear. Now Megwadesk looked at his lifeless net and wished he had his eel-spear with him.

"Ah, but why imagine I'd be doing good in spearing eels, eh?" he asked. "When a man's unlucky in one thing he's lucky in nothing 'tall."

He thought about the games he had played with the men at the hall for the past three evenings, hoping to make some money gambling. He would have done better throwing the dice into the river the first day he got them.

Megwadesk felt trapped and he wanted to tear away at the web around him. The air was sticky and suffocating. The trees were too close; the hills were too crowding; the clouds were too low; the river was too narrow; and every sound was too immediate. But where else, he wondered, was there for him to go? Messkíg reservation was ringed by white squatters who had seized vast tracts of Indian land. All the Micmac shacks were huddled into a few acres.

Megwadesk saw the doe raise her head and stand stock still. Suddenly he felt something else, something like a sinister whisper drifting over the water. Instantly, his frustration was replaced by an unaccountable yet familiar alarm. Megwadesk froze. The doe across the river pricked its ears and sniffed the air. She nudged the fawn's rump and turned around to reenter the woods. The mallards quit their nasal chatter and paddled into the reeds to hide. The loons shouted to each other and took to the air. The owl fell silent. A thick, nefarious hush cloaked and muffled the air. Nothing moved, nothing stirred. The night – and every creature of the night – held its breath. A meteorite streaked silently out of the Milky Way and as silently went out.

Then it happened! A tug from the bottom plunged the outermost float on Skoltch's net into the water, and all along the net a shoreward ripple set the other floats bouncing. Another tug came from the centre. And another closer to shore. Soon the water around the net was a collision of ripples, a choppy, crowded scrambling. The floats bobbed in longer and longer intervals while the splashing sharpened.

Megwadesk knew that schools of bass were nosing their gills into the threaded mesh. He looked at his net. He saw not a tremble, not the least vibration. He thought of how the animals always fled just before Skoltch's net became a commotion of panic. Megwadesk gaped. It seemed that the world was now a dream. Each night when this happened, no matter how often he had seen it, the world of water and woods dissolved into a waking, maddening dream. Each night when this happened, Megwadesk was stung by the memory of when he was eleven years old and he caught nothing more than a few beavers on his grandfather's trapline.

Megwadesk let the alder stick slip from his fingers. He absently sheathed his knife, not noticing he had sharpened the stick on both ends.

Then he watched for an hour, as the net that was not his, grew heavy with bass. The net became so weighted it suddenly submerged and a final nub of undulation wiped the surface, polishing the water again. The breath of malevolence vanished from the water. Chigdeg. A natural silence returned – the kind of silence that was alive with the stir of insects and the usual nocturnal scraping of dead leaves in the bushes; a silence that would cannon over miles of hills the butting of moose racks against oaks or the slapping of beaver tails flat against the muck. Megwadesk saw his advantage in this night so robust with potential volume.

Surely, he thought, *I'll hear Skoltch blundering down the hill, eh, long before he reaches the shore. Anyway, I've never seen'm 'tall to come down 'n' check his net before morning – the lazy lout!*

And then he thought again, *Well, does a man who don't keep an eye on his net deserve such a haul? Moquá. I got no intentions of taking from his catch, eh. Alls I wanna do is just go 'n' see what it looks like. Yep. Might be some flounder 'n' crabs've knotted his net. Tangled mesh ain't no good 'tall, eh. It's got to be untangled. Éhe, I'll just go and check his net for him.*

He took three steps down the quick bank and bounded onto the deck of his boat. The soles of his boots touched down with all the grace of a pair of granite blocks. POCK! CLUMP!

"Oops!" he muttered, crouching down cat-like and clenching his teeth, his arms winging out to his sides and his head quickly cocking in and out of several different angles like the head of an alarmed grouse.

"Oops!" he repeated, as if to say, "Easy now!"

The frowning wavelets fanning from the corners of his flat-bottomed boat almost coerced him into making an outright apology.

"I just want to see what he's got," he muttered sheepishly.

In the distance he heard a fiddle playing a slow waltz and it sounded sad. For a second he accompanied the tune with imagined guitar chords. Then the song faded.

"Yes, my dear," he whispered. "Our luck's gonna change tonight."

He carefully lifted the anchor from the grass and set it down inside the boat, in a box containing an old net. Beside the box were three empty crates, a shovel, an oyster rake, a pail, and a hammer. A cast-iron pot was hidden under the deck and along the length of one side of the scow lay sharpened poles of various lengths. Megwadesk scooped up the end of the longest pole sticking out over the deck and walked with it, holding it horizontally at waist level, to the rear of the boat. He resembled a tight-rope walker, stepping lightly as he did. He stopped and stood near the transom end for a long time, trying to catch his breath without breathing too hard. His breathing deafened him.

Why'm I so nervous, anyway, he wondered, *when alls I'm doing's looking out for my neighbour? Éhe. I'm just gonna disentangle his net of crabs. That way his mesh'll be free to catch more bass.*

He wiped his forehead and face with the left sleeve of his plaid shirt. A cool breeze nudged the floats of his net.

I'm only doing what's right, he thought, and he purposely stamped his right foot on the plywood floor of the boat. His loud stomp echoed upriver and downriver.

Amudj! he thought. *I've only got good intentions! Why, Nisgam nuduid, I should row out there whistling 'n' singing alls I please! I should slap my paddles in the water like I don't care 'tall! Éhe! I'll do that!*

Megwadesk pressed the heavy end of his pole in the sand and pushed on it, releasing the prow of the boat from the flattened grass. The base of the transom gurgled and the chin of the craft skimmed over the water as it swung out in an arc.

Megwadesk glanced at the crates in his boat. He thought, *Them crates've been empty for six days now. Six awful days! Now say, if I clean his net of crabs 'n' flounder 'n' driftwood 'n' mudsuckers 'n', hell, all those other miserable things that take up space or tear gaping holes into nets, well, then, don't that deserve some payment in turn? An' ain't it traditional for Micmacs to share their catch, anyhow? Why, sure it is! But ain't Skoltch broken this tradition time and time again? Yes, 'cause alls he does is look out for hisself and no one else 'tall! Isn't that so? Well, then,*

13

who can say anything if I, in turn, broke, say, a rule or two, huh?

The empty crates he gazed on demanded answers to his questions.

Skoltch borrows from me lots of times, he thought, *so if I took a few bass, well, geez, wouldn't that be the same as borrowing from him? An' all this stuff about witchery – it's just foolishness anyway! I've got nothing to fear 'tall.*

Still he remembered how Mimi kept one chair beside the door, a chair she offered any visitor who entered the house. To all appearances the chair was no different from any other chair, but its bottom side had been specially treated with salt so that a witch or a warlock would automatically refuse it. He or she would suddenly smile and perhaps say, "Oh, I'm sorry, dear, but I really can't stay," or, if an elder, he or she might ask for a "softer" chair. Megwadesk knew that there were many ways to avoid such a specially treated chair. Mimi claimed evil people were instinctively averse to such a chair because it drained their power.

"I want to know who not to open my door and my heart to," Mimi once said.

Megwadesk knew that people believed in a buowin, a man of evil powers, who gained influence over people by winning favours and gifts from them. A buowin won sympathy only to use sympathy against those who were kind to him.

Megwadesk forced a chuckle and thought, *But what does Mimi know, anyhow? She's just a girl who's heard too many silly ghost stories, eh.*

As Megwadesk poled his boat out to the channel's edge, the breeze gained strength. The night grew cooler. Megwadesk drifted alongside his empty net momentarily, then he took a seat and rowed, swinging around the stake that marked the end of his net. Megwadesk did not splash his paddles nor did he sing. Instead he listened intently above the stealth of his rowing. He listened for footsteps or for twigs snapping but all he could hear in the stillness was his mother saying, "Doing evil doesn't pay. It all comes back eventually. That's why witches suffer in the end." His mother had always introduced her tales of witchery with those words.

"I know, I know," Megwadesk grumbled. "I just wanna

see his catch 'n' maybe have his luck rub off on me."

The hoot of an owl startled him. Its sudden call felt like the hand of winter gripping his heart.

"Boys oh boys, you frightened me!" he hissed at the owl.

Megwadesk had to pause to catch his breath. A swarm of fire-flies streamed from the bushes along the shore and up the bank towards the woods. He rowed again and aimed for the stake that marked the end of his neighbour's net.

"Hush!" he hissed at the wavelets slapping against the floor of his boat's prow.

With a powerful thrust from his oars, he sent his grey boat gliding towards the sunken net. He stood up and faced the deck of his boat to grab the approaching stake. To his horror, as he stood up and turned around, he found himself dwarfed beneath the floodlight of a fast-clearing moon. The full moon of olive green appeared bloated and squat like a bullfrog hunkered on the clouds – and the rush of the light, casting broad slices of gleam across the waters and an inescapable brilliance over the entire area, threw Megwadesk back to his seat and back to his oars.

"Gisúlk! The moon, the light!" he gasped.

He hastily back-paddled his left oar and forward-paddled his right oar, spinning around in one spot. Then he shot his craft beachward towards the rock anchoring his net to shore.

"I better get home," he said. "I better get home. My honey can get frightened all by her lonesome. Yep, women are cowards sometimes – I better get home."

Megwadesk beached. He tossed the anchor on the bank and leapt right after it. As he hurried up the hill and vanished from the riverbank setting, another rack of easterly clouds crowded the moon. And soon it was dark again.

Chapter Two

Tiny Moccasins

With morning came rain. It began to pour before sunrise. Quick as anger, lightning streaked. The skyquake cracked dazzling fault-lines that opened and shut over Messkíg reservation. Seismic growls of thunder followed. Inside their cramped house, Megwadesk and Mimi listened to the rain on the rooftop.

To Megwadesk, the rain drummed like thousands of worried fingers. The thunder pained his head. The sky crackled and snapped like bones that were being broken by the jaws of a ravenous beast. A fantastic boom blasted into the pines – an explosive shout thrown from the lungs of bruised clouds – knocking off innumerable swollen rain drops that had gathered on the tips of green bristles.

Megwadesk thought about his dream of the night before. No sooner had he fallen asleep, he dreamed of a rabid dog attacking him. He woke up exhausted and too scared to fall back to sleep. For about a week now, animals had attacked him in his dreams. One night it had been a bear; another night a huge horse. He had not told Mimi about his dreams. He knew that Mimi, who knew much about herbs and plants and the many old beliefs that went with medicine, would interpret the dreams to mean somebody was working a hex on him. He did not want to hear that. Not now. Not when thunder, lightning, rain and darkness held a most unfair advantage over reason.

He felt uneasy about the dreams, but he still believed that everything his people usually considered to be of ghostly origin could be explained as a trick of nature and he wanted this idea to grow strong enough in his mind to en-able him to overcome his fears.

It's our silly old beliefs, eh, that keep us from getting anywhere, he thought. *Everything's taboo with us, eh. An' these beliefs go deeper than the head. Nisgam, just look at me, eh! Last night I could've taken advantage of Skoltch's net but I ran away instead! An' why? 'Cause I was 'fraid of the spirits getting back at me! An' Nisgam nuduid, even though I know in my head that it's all nonsense, I can't get past what I was raised to believe! Or take a look at that quill-basket there, that's full of Mimi's rocks. I could crack 'em rocks open 'n' sell the crystals inside 'em for lots of money, eh. Oh, Nisgam, éq! White people'll pay lots of money for 'em. But Mimi can't get past what she was raised to believe. So she won't sell 'em 'tall 'cause they're s'posed to be magical! Humph!*

Megwadesk leaned his right elbow on the little table that stood before the window. He rested his chin on the bowl of his right palm and rolled his sad-looking eyes around, avoiding the question he saw in Mimi's eyes.

Lately Mimi's behaviour was a mystery to him. She could exchange an emotional face with its opposite quicker than it took a heron to spike a minnow. Yet she was more industrious than ever. Everywhere that Megwadesk turned his eyes there was the evidence of Mimi's tireless artistry. Hanging over the table from the roofbeam – now being rocked by a thunderclap – were a pair of tiny newly-made moccasins with a little rattle between them. *'Nother good luck charm,* Megwadesk thought. Complete sets of birchbark baskets decorated with dyed porcupine quills sat on the shelves that ran above the indoor stash of firewood. Half-completed curtains draped the little sewing table. And in the corner was a burlap bag filled with freshly-harvested delicious, young potatoes and turnips so juicy their peelings came off in one piece like the bark of a year-dead tree.

Dark spots under his eyes made Megwadesk look sad and weary. The calloused fingers of his left hand, yellowed by many mornings of stoking his white stone pipe which he had been missing for several days now, scratched the hair stubs on his jaw and then crawled over to his left ear lobe to play with it the way a magician's fingers played with a coin. Seeing, from the corner of his eye, Mimi pacing the floor made Megwadesk nervous. He almost went to the corner to retrieve his guitar and busy his fingers on the strings, even though music was not in his heart just then. Absently, he brushed his fingers through his thick, glossy hair. He wished he had his pipe. He wondered where he could have lost it.

"Have you seen my pipe anywhere, Mimi?" he asked.

"Is that all you worry about?" Mimi replied. She strode to the fifty-gallon oil drum, which had been converted into a wood-burning stove, and kicked the vent door shut.

"Na! No use burning more wood," she snapped. "I've done all my cooking for today!"

She brushed her hair from her face and glared at Megwadesk. She wore one long skirt over another long skirt. Usually the rustling of her bright blue skirts accompanied any of her movements but the pummelling rain drowned out all sounds.

Megwadesk thought, *Not again, please, not 'nother one of your sudden fits.*

His stomach growled. Their breakfast had been turnips with salt pork, a few potatoes and weak tea. Their thin, pan-fried bread had been spread with salted lard instead of butter. All the money Mimi had made from her porcupine quill baskets over the winter had gone into building supplies for their new home. It was now up to Megwadesk to get them through the summer and fall. Megwadesk had promised her that he would buy a stove from the extra he made in fishing this year. But instead of salmon or boiled lobster, their only meat for the past week had been thin slices of salted pork.

Now a bucket behind the stove caught rain water dripping from a leak in the roof. The tiny house felt damp and cool. Another puddle had formed near the door. They had not been able to afford roofing shingles and the tarpaper was already tearing in places.

"What kind of gardener could I call myself if I planted and harvested only one food like, say, potatoes?" Mimi sarcastically wondered aloud. "See? If I hadn't planted turnips, we'd be in poor shape, I tell you. Nisgam nuduid!"

"I know, I know," Megwadesk muttered. "Thought I could count on my bass net, eh, but – I promise – tonight I won't depend on it 'tall. Tonight I'll go spearing eels instead."

"Eíoqa! Lots of good that'll do us now," Mimi flared. "All this rain is going to muddy up the river! You'll be lucky to see two inches into the water! Nisgam! What do you plan to do? Do you think you can strike anywhere you like and hit an eel just like playing Pin the Tail on the Donkey?"

"I'll go out to ykdánug, eh, out by the ocean."

"What for? You won't see a thing there either. It's windy and rough."

"But it's clear there," Megwadesk answered, trying to keep the growl out his voice. "I'll just stay inside the break-waters, eh, where it's calmer. Alls I need is one good night of fishing."

Megwadesk stared at the statue of St. Anne that stood beside an empty picnic basket on the top shelf. St. Anne's Day celebrations, when – among other activities – families and couples would go out on the boats to enjoy picnics downriver, were coming up in a week and they had no money. He knew Mimi was right. What was more, Megwadesk knew he could not spear eels, even in perfect weather. His cousin, Talon, had not yet returned the eel-spear he had borrowed over three weeks ago. For all that Megwadesk knew, Talon was still camped by the breakwa-ters. Mimi knew nothing about this arrangement. Megwadesk never told Mimi when he let people borrow from him because Mimi always got upset. And Mimi got upset more easily now than ever before. Megwadesk did not know how to account for her mood swings.

"Jee hover Moses' sakes! Last night, and the night be-fore, and the night before the night before – all those per-fectly calm nights – you had all that time to spear eels!" Mimi yelled. "But what did you do instead? You sat by the bank and stared at your godforsaken net! Nisgam, Máli!"

"Boys oh boys, will you quit it!" Megwadesk fired back, half-rising from his seat. "What's it with you, anyway? I can't remember the last time you didn't complain 'bout something or 'nother twice before noon! Nisgam nuduid, the way you go on sometimes you'd think we're the only people having it rough, eh!"

"Quit it? You want me to quit it? Lately you act more dead than alive! If you want me off your case, mister, you better start using your head for a change!"

Megwadesk eased back on his seat and said, "Oh, I'd say I use my head more 'an you! You're the one who talks 'bout some boogie man sneaking 'round here! Well, tell me dear, has that boogie man been 'round lately, eh? I never see its tracks 'tall. Must be a ghost, eh!"

"So you didn't believe me, huh?" Mimi looked stricken. "Maybe you'd be pretty worked up, too, if somebody was always prowling around where you are! And maybe you'd feel pretty lousy if you're partner didn't do nothing about it, didn't even believe you!"

Megwadesk saw that Mimi was on the verge of tears. He wished he had never ridiculed her reports about somebody creeping around their house when he was away. But he had checked around the house each time for any signs of a prowler and had not seen so much as a matted patch of grass. He was sure that Mimi had only imagined things. He wondered if the pressures of living together as a common-law couple were getting to her. *Maybe,* he thought, *she's not happy with me. Maybe she figures she made a mistake, eh.*

Mimi suddenly felt exhausted. Her jaw slackened and her forehead muscles crawled beneath the drained skin. She leaned back on the stove, pressing her palm on the edge of it for an instant, before she jumped.

"Oh, shit!"

"Careful, sugar," Megwadesk warned belatedly.

Mimi faced the stove, turning her profile to Megwadesk. She watched a blister swell on her palm. She sighed and her expression acquired a child-like bewilderment. She wiped her face with her hands and then lowered her hands around her throat, where she rested one hand over the other. Her arms rested over her breasts.

"Megwadesk," she murmured. "I'm pregnant."

The din of the torrent distorted her words.

"I know. An' you got every right to be angry, my sugar," Megwadesk returned. "But, I promise, I'll go spearing eels tonight, even if I have to go all the way past the breakwaters."

"Megwadesk!" Mimi said louder, wheeling around to face him squarely. "I said I am pregnant!" And now her pupils dilated and the lustrous blackness of her eyes swarmed with emotions. Then suddenly her eyes sparkled with laughter.

"You mean you really didn't know, you silly?" she asked, smiling with the inner ends of her eyebrows pressed up.

Megwadesk stared at her.

"We have to talk to the minister tonight," said Mimi. "He'll be here and we don't have anything to offer him!"

Megwadesk slowly rose to his feet and then announced in a mechanical voice, "I'll go borrow some food from Skoltch, dear."

"But be careful!"

Megwadesk turned around and was about to rush outside, when the words about Mimi's pregnancy that had sent a shiver into his being turned from the north and started blowing in from the south. Then the words became a southwest wind, ticklish and fatuous, and Megwadesk grinned foolishly and turned to Mimi and laughed and said, "Nisgam nuduid, woman, we're gonna have a feast! Bana, don't worry 'bout a thing!"

Megwadesk strode over to Mimi and hugged her.

"I really had no idea," he said.

Mimi pressed him closer, her full and silky lips kissing the hollow just over his left collarbone. "You're such a fool not to have guessed," she said, "but you're my fool."

Megwadesk nuzzled his face into her lush and soft hair. Mimi included juice boiled from fir needles in her shampoo recipe. He gulped a great breath of her forest fragrance and slowly exhaled.

"Mégadu welamul aqq gesalul goqwei," he whispered, and then he blushed and pressed her shoulders away from him. He had said, "I find you incredibly beautiful and I love you so." Something he never before told her.

Megwadesk always complimented Mimi by saying such and such a thing looked beautiful on her. And the closest he had come to the word "gesalul," was to say he wanted her to be with him in everything he did.

Megwadesk stepped back from Mimi and said, "Open the vent 'n' throw some more wood in the stove. I'll be back with food! Mostly vegetables, right?"

"Yes, for him. But why don't you go see your mother instead of Skoltch?" Mimi advised.

His parents had so strongly objected to his common-law union with Mimi that hot words had been exchanged between Megwadesk and his father. Since then, Mimi had felt responsible for this family rupture.

Megwadesk answered, "Skoltch'll help us, 'cause he's

borrowed so many times from us."

There was no point in seeing Mimi's mother for help. She struggled alone with her little ones, while her husband worked in a large fishing boat near Grand Manan. Besides, Megwadesk would have viewed calling on her as an admittance that he was an unworthy husband for her daughter.

"No, don't go to that place, please!" Mimi insisted.

"But why not, sugar? Skoltch borrows from us all the time. Why shouldn't he help me out now?"

"Don't go there, dear! I'm sure that old woman's evil!"

"Who? His mum?"

"Éhe! She came here a week ago, while you were down by the river. She wanted me to teach her about stone medicine, about the crystal stones and their powers and all the rituals that I learned from my godmother. She said she could use it to help more people than I did."

"Now come on - "

"No, listen! You know that people say she has medicine – especially with bushes and thorns – but I know she's not just a healer! Nisgam nuduid, she's evil, too. I offered her that chair, the one that's specially treated with salt, and she refused it. I insisted that she sit on it and she got really mad at me! I wouldn't let her sit on anything else and she finally exploded! She drilled her eyes into mine and said, 'Well, we'll see whose medicine is stronger! I'll give a you a licking with my switches, girl, if you don't soon learn to respect your elders!' That's exactly what she said! That was a week ago. I didn't tell you about it because lately you've been making fun of our people's medicine ways!"

"Oh, come on, Mimi, you're not gonna let that nonsense scare you, eh? Geez, I wish you didn't believe in that stuff 'tall! We could make some money from them rocks you got."

"Oh, don't say that! I'm just worried about you. She might try to get to me by getting at you. Has anything strange happened to you?"

"No, nothing. Don't worry about her, Mimi. She's just trying to scare you, eh, 'cause she knows you believe in all that stuff."

"Well, how come Skoltch is getting fish and you're not? Aren't you guys set near the same spot?"

"Hey, fish are just funny like that, eh! Geez, cut this stuff out, eh! I'm all right. I'm doing just fine, eh! Now come on, quit putting a damper on the good news. Holy smokes, we should be celebrating!"

"Here – take this basket, then," Mimi said, extending a picnic basket to him.

"No. I'll soon return with more than that basket can hold," he replied. "Oh, yeah, more than that basket can hold, all right! I know Skoltch! He's a good guy!"

Megwadesk kissed Mimi and then he strode to the door. Next to the door, on a half-sunk, rusted, spike, hung his woollen, hooded jacket and his navy-blue cap. He put his jacket on and roughly flattened the cap over his head. He opened the door. Lightning flashed and Mimi heard Megwadesk laugh before thunder shook the small house and the door slammed shut.

The silver crucifix over the door blew off the hook and Mimi rushed forward to catch it just in time. Since the nail over the door was too high for her to reach, she looked for another place to hang the crucifix. Beside the door on a brass hook was suspended a small poem framed in a wreath of sweetgrass. The tiny lettering read:

I was a volcano once,
shouldering mountain night,
lungs filled with
the shout of lava
longing
longing
to burn air
with ardent words.

The poem was signed, "For our new friendship; may God bless us all – Matthew Severman." Mimi hung the crucifix over it.

Chapter Three

Witchery of the Worst Kind

Megwadesk raced across the clearing in front of the house. The cold drops that sprinkled his neck and collar and trickled down his back could not dispel from his mind the picture of Mimi's gorgeous face. Her hair was so thick and yet so soft. Her narrow face accentuated the smooth brown curves of her cheekbones, and her large and deep, dark eyes seemed larger and richer and more promising. And just now, her plump lips had looked even juicier! The underside of her arms had been so warm, too, and as velvety as the bottom side of a young and tender hazel leaf!

She must have felt so alone, he thought, recalling the many times he espied her knitted brows as she worked on one of her many projects.

Then he rejoiced, *Oquetédud! We're going to have a baby! Edynaha! We'll have lots of babies, eh! Lots! An' I'll pray they survive! But first, we'll get married, eh, just like we planned! The preacher'll visit tonight! Mimi'll make a good feast for him!*

He knew that, as far as Mimi was concerned, the idea of the local Catholic priest, Father Colérique, uniting them in marriage was out of the question. Mimi had already told Megwadesk that she hoped the new preacher, Mr. Severman, would perform their wedding ceremony. Mimi hated Father Colérique because she blamed him for having the stigma of an illegitimate child attached to her. Mimi had told Megwadesk that when Mimi's mother was pregnant with her, Mimi's mother and father, who had been living in common-law – contrary to Church laws – had asked Father Colérique to unite them but the priest had refused. He said the couple had lived in sin and they, consequently, had to bear the shame they brought onto themselves.

"The Church doesn't conduct ceremonies of convenience," he told Mimi's parents. "I won't be rushed into uniting two people without the proper preparations, and without allowing the young couple the appropriate period of deliberation. Divorce is an abomination and I won't marry a couple unless I'm certain they understand the significance of marriage vows."

Mimi said her parents had married only after she was born. She grew up struggling against the label of bastard child. Her hatred for the priest was fuelled by his attitude towards her. Father Colérique, she said, considered illegitimate children products of sin. The priest often preached against promiscuity and common-law unions by using illegitimate children as examples of "bad fruit."

Megwadesk remembered that there were only three illegitimate girls in Messkíg when Mimi was a young girl. He knew that the other two had been crushed at an early age by the prejudice they had encountered. Their drinking and sleeping around had inspired countless sermons. Mimi told Megwadesk that she was sure her unbroken spirit had incensed the priest. Instead of submitting to the priest's low expectations, Mimi proved herself exceptional in every challenge she undertook. She learned from her mother how to read and write Micmac and then taught herself how to read and write in English, too. She picked up fiddle playing from her father and eventually became the favourite entertainer in the monthly square dances. But it was making birchbark baskets, decorated with dyed porcupine quills, that was Mimi's specialty. She made baskets year-round and sold most of them just before Christmas. She was so good at finding markets for her excellent work that other women in Messkíg grew to depend on her for selling their work, too.

Although Mimi had shown that an illegitimate child need not grow up to be another "black sheep," she had told Megwadesk, before they had begun living together, that when she became pregnant, she would not allow what happened to her to happen to her child. She would not bring an illegitimate child into the world. She would get married first she said, even if a judge performed the ceremony. When a missionary of a Protestant denomination, Mr. Severman, who had worked many years in western Canada, began to frequent Messkíg two months ago, he found a friendly audience in Mimi and Megwadesk's tiny home. Megwadesk recalled it was then that the idea of converting to a new faith had struck Mimi.

Oh, don't you worry about it, Mimi, dear, Megwadesk thought, *'cause we'll get Mr. Severman to marry us all right. Yep, we'll give him a good feast tonight, eh, 'cause Skoltch'll help me out with the food. An' Father Colérique, why, he'll soon find out that he ain't no longer the only holy roller in town!*

Megwadesk reached the woods but even the shelter of dense trees did little to restrain the torrent. He ran through the woods on a narrow trail leading towards Skoltch's house. This old trail was lower on the hill than the road he was working on. A thick coat of mud stuck on the soles of his boots. The hollow of the footpath now served as a minor tributary. Megwadesk tried to stay on the grassy shoulders but sometimes clumps of willow bushes or maple saplings narrowed the trail, forcing him to splash through the streaming water. Lightning flashed so regularly and intensely that it gave Megwadesk a headache. Between flashes, floating puddles of violet and blue blinded him. At those moments, he stumbled into bushes or tramped into ruts hidden under the rushing water. All around him the woods resounded with detonations. Frequently the rumblings throbbed right through his jogging body.

Megwadesk approached a clearing. For a moment, he felt better, once he saw the cemetery. Past the cemetery, with its white wooden crosses, began a good wide road. But as he sprinted through the middle of the burial ground, he saw many tiny and stony graves from which no clumps of grass sprouted yet. Measles. It had been measles the past winter and spring; the year before it had been double pneumonia.

Will our people, Megwadesk wondered, *ever stop dying from diseases?* He thought of how every time a new scourge had decimated the population of Messkíg, the white people of Trenton had treated Indians like rabid dogs. To reach the breakwaters, the summer haven they called ykdánug, the people of Messkíg had to go past the bridge connecting the north part of Trenton with its south part. The townfolk of Trenton would wait on the bridge with rocks. They would beat most of the Indians back.

"Stay in your fucken reserve!" the townfolk raged. "We don't want your fucken diseases!"

And the stone throwers shouted other things, - filthy things the Micmacs lacked words for in their language. Only those with short but very wide sails managed to slip past the bridge. The rest had to skulk past it at night, and it was humiliating to be reduced to slinking around in one's country. The last child to die of measles, died in early May, but the rocks kept falling all summer.

Pestilence reduced Messkíg to thirty-four shacks ringed by white squatters. Megwadesk recalled that it didn't matter, either, how often the chief and the people petitioned the Crown to get squatters off reserve land. The government did nothing. Indians could not vote and squatters could. Megwadesk knew that already the squatters claimed to have cleared many old Micmac lots, justifying their theft of the land with the lie that they tilled the land and made it useful while Indians had done nothing with it. But Megwadesk knew the truth. He remembered when his uncle cleared land upriver and planted potatoes in the spring twelve years ago. During the summer his uncle went to Maine to sell potato baskets to the farmers. When he returned to harvest his crop, a white man was on his lot. The white man thrust a rifle to his face and told him to leave. So the people wrote more petitions. But the government waited, perhaps hoping the Micmacs would be extinct within a few more decades.

Yes, we'll have many children, Megwadesk thought. *Twelve, at least. An' maybe half'll survive, eh. I pray this one does!*

He thought about the bridge again and, in a way, he did not miss hauling in great catches of bass. A dealer, who did not turn Indian fishermen away, lived on the other side of Trenton. It was lucrative business for him. Since nobody else bought fish from Indians, he could get their fish and pay less than half the price for it. But first the Micmac fishermen had to get past the bridge. Megwadesk did not miss the stone throwers. Nor did he miss the indignity of knowing he was being cheated by a dealer who constantly slammed things about and always reminded the Micmacs, "I don't have to do this, you know."

Megwadesk reached the far end of the cemetery. He took

a wide berth around the twenty-feet tall, white, wooden cross standing close to the road. He feared there was a good chance of lightning striking the cross – for the cross was the only prominent landmark on the open area – and he did not want to be close when shock surged through it. Veering from the cross, he had no choice but to leap over the fresh grave of an adult. He couldn't remember the death of an adult in recent months so, for an instant, the grave puzzled him. Racing on, Megwadesk suddenly remembered that Peter Algumid, with a party of men, had moved Old Set-Ból's body from the swamp to the consecrated ground.

The story they tell now 'bout Old Set-Ból coming back to haunt the priest – well, that's just proof, eh, that our people'll believe any foolish thing you tell 'em, Megwadesk told himself.

Megwadesk thought about the story Peter Algumid, the church keeper, had told him. Old Set-Ból had died four years ago. All the people remembered Old Set-Ból as a kind and gentle man. Megwadesk remembered that the people used to call him a ginab, a man of mysterious and good powers. He was a generous man but the priest had still found fault with him. According to Peter Algumid, Father Colérique had been angry with Old Set-Ból because the influential old man had never honoured the priest with a confession. When Old Set-Ból died, Father Colérique banished his body to the swamps. Although he was a Catholic, Old Set-Ból had never done his Easter duty. Suicide victims, couples who lived common-law, and people who never did their Easter duties could not be buried in consecrated ground. That was the law. Everybody knew it. The law was severe and because of this severity the people never applied it. So they had warned Father Colérique not to banish Old Set-Ból to the swamps but the priest had not relented.

Megwadesk recalled what the local gossips said about the events that had followed after Old Set-Ból had been buried in the swamps. It was all nonsense to Megwadesk but according to Peter Algumid and other lovers of tall tales, Father Colérique soon changed. The priest became haggard and nervous. His hair turned grey. He became a recluse, locking himself in his house. For several years he kept his troubles close to his heart. Then one day he supposedly confessed to Peter Algumid that a ghost was haunting him. And the ghost gave him no rest.

Peter Algumid told how he asked Father Colérique if he had seen the ghost. Father Colérique said yes, that he had seen it, that it stood outside his screen door knocking one night, water dripping from his moon-lit hair. And the ghost followed him everywhere. He had seen it on the farm in Gaspé when he went home to visit his parents. He had seen it during his pilgrimage to St-Anne-de-Beaupré. He had seen it when he spent two weeks in New York. He said the ghost always smelled of cattails and tamaracks; rushes and moss. At first, the ghost appeared only monthly. Then it appeared weekly.

"Old Set-Ból won't give me any rest!" Father Colérique cried. "Each time I see him, his body has decomposed even more! And he tells me, I too, am rotting just as surely as he! Look at me! Am I not withering? Am I not gaunt? But, I tell you, I cannot look into the mirror at all these days! I don't see myself as I am in the mirror! I see my skin peeling off, my teeth exposed, and my eyeballs sunken into my skull!

"People knock on my door and I won't answer unless they call me and I recognize their voices! I won't answer because I'm afraid it might be *him! He* knocks on my door and on my windows every night! And when it pours and thunders, I hear him in every corner of the house, tapping, tapping, tapping! Oh, no prayer – nothing holy – can give me help! I have been banished from God – condemned to purgatory! The people are angry with me! I don't attend wakes! I don't visit the sick! They are angry but they don't know what I am going through!"

Peter Algumid said that he had known then that they had to find Old Set-Ból's body and rebury it in the cemetery. Peter Algumid and a party of men searched for his grave but in the intervening years, the swamp had sprouted alders where the trails had been. Everything looked different. For another year the swamp kept Old Set-Ból's grave hidden and so for one more year – the story had it – the priest suffered nightly horrors. Finally, this very spring they found the grave and they dug up Old Set-Ból's bones and returned them to the village. The people held one night of wake and then conducted an official funeral the next morning, complete with Father Colérique's blessings.

Peter Algumid said the night after Old Set-Ból was reburied, there was a knock on Father Colérique's door. Father Colérique cheerfully answered the door only to be shocked to find Old Set-Ból standing in the dark porch, his soulless eyes blinking and glittering in the shadows.

"Will this nightmare never end?" Father Colérique wondered out loud.

Then Old Set-Ból, after thanking him for allowing his spirit to continue its journey to the next world, assured the priest he would not trouble him again. As Old Set-Ból turned to walk away, Father Colérique noticed his clothes were in excellent condition and his face and his body looked healthy; he was not decomposing. It was said that Father Colérique now slept soundly through the nights. Megwadesk, however, doubted that anything could humble such a hard man as Father Colérique.

These are the kinds of silly stories they dream up, eh, Megwadesk thought, *just to get back at a priest they've always been scared of. The priest gets old, gets grey hair, starts to stutter, so they explain it with something as foolish as that! Humph! Maybe it makes 'em feel good, eh, to imagine somebody they've always been scared of as going through something so scary. In their way of thinking, the story puts the priest in his place – even if the story ain't got no truth to it 'tall! Boys oh boys, even Mimi told me, "I don't think he'll banish anyone to the swamps any more. I'd like to see him banish me, boys! Nisgam nuduid, I'll come back and make the rest of his hair fall out!"*

Thinking about Old Set-Ból's cadaver, however, made Megwadesk's mind turn to nightmarish images. The horrors he used to feel as a child when thinking about judgement day came back to him. Cemeteries always made him think about judgement day, but now the nightmare seemed more vivid and imminent than ever. Eternal damnation did not scare him at all. It was always the thought of seeing graves opening up and millions of corpses stepping out to receive judgement that truly horrified him. He could not imagine anything more revolting than the earth regurgitating its most recent morsels of half-digested generations. Men, women and children would stand up on that day with clogs of fat, white maggots spilling out of their mouths.

Oh, it's insane! he thought. *How will I dare look at my grand-parents, eh? Why would any god demand such a crazy sight?*

He could not see a divine hand in the matter. To Megwadesk, judgement day was witchery of the worst kind. It was either the whiteman's Christian world or the old Indian beliefs that were correct but both of them had aspects that revolted him. Megwadesk ran even faster to get to the road. His collar was drenched and his woollen jacket was heavy. On the flat rocks of the road he stomped the mud off his boots and then he jogged up the steep hill where Skoltch's house stood. The house could not be seen from the road. Stands of knotty jackpine and fir hid the sharp-pitched roof of the house. A narrow driveway curved into these trees. Walls of water repeatedly sliced the world from him but he was sure he was on the correct path.

No sooner was Megwadesk under the branches of the nearest pine, when a savagely gnarling dog came charging towards him. The sheltering pines broke the sheets of rain and Megwadesk got a good look at the attacking beast. The broad and powerfully built dog was black with patches of rusty brown on its breast and hinds. It's demented eyes blazed yellowish. The tiniest of red dots were its pupils. Megwadesk instantly shook off half his jacket, freeing his right arm. The dog charged on. Megwadesk kept on the left sleeve of his jacket. He thrust out his left arm and hastily wrapped the rest of his jacket around the sleeve.

Lightning exploded just then, freezing the image of the dog before it leaped, its fangs gleaming with foam and a spray of saliva whipping out of its maw. The lightning dazed Megwadesk. In its wake came a blinding swarm of splotches. Megwadesk waited for the impact of the dog's attack. Before his vision cleared, he felt the powerful jaws lock around his wrapped forearm. Almost instantaneously the dog's weight knocked him back.

Megwadesk thought about unsheathing the fishing knife belted to his right hip and slashing the dog's throat. Still, just the realization that he had this option made him feel more in control. *Anyway,* he thought, *how can I ask a favour from Skoltch, eh, after killing his dog?*

Megwadesk let the dog jerk around his forearm. He knew the worst thing he could do was kick the dog. The dog would release its grip from his well-padded forearm and crunch into his unprotected leg. Megwadesk yelled at the dog. The jacket unrolled a bit and soon the dog was tugging at one sleeve while Megwadesk tugged at the other.

A huge man appeared at the bend of the driveway. The dog tugged harder and Megwadesk heard his jacket rip. He cursed and wished now he had slit the dog's throat. Nothing was worth the mangling of his favourite jacket. Although the man was round, he moved with the surprising grace and speed of a retired boxer. The huge man ran to the dog. All in one motion, he grabbed the dog by its scruff and tossed it into the ditch. Swearing and yelling, the big man ran to the dog again and kicked its muzzle. The dog yelped and then beat a retreat.

"Get back to the house!" the towering man roared at the dog, vigorously stabbing a fleshy finger back the way he had just come.

"Boys oh boys, you should keep that damn dog on a leash!" Megwadesk shouted, rubbing his arm. "I got half a mind to get my rifle 'n' shoot that bitch! I should've slit 'er throat the moment it jumped me! I should never've shown no mercy 'tall!"

The heavy man turned and addressed Megwadesk, "She's never been like that! Never seen her that ugly! Come on in! She won't trouble you no more! Come on, I said! Let's get out of this downpour!"

The burly man waved his arm as he sprinted off and yelled again, "Come on, boy!"

They hastened around the bend and the steep-roofed house appeared. The dog hid under the porch steps. Just before the two men hurried into the porch, Megwadesk caught sight of the small barn off to the side, partly hidden by more trees. A light was burning in the barn. Megwadesk wondered if Skoltch was bootlegging again. No music or laughter came from the barn, though.

Megwadesk, with his cousin, Talon, who sometimes drank hard, once attended a party at the barn. Megwadesk had played rhythm guitar to the fiddling of three old-timers. Only musicians who had agreed to entertain the whole night received free booze. Megwadesk remembered how jealously Old Molly, Skoltch's mother, guarded a well in a dark recess off to the back. She had worn an eye-patch over her right eye. Throughout the party the old woman never left her post. Megwadesk thought she was perhaps timid or shy, not desiring to get too close to the revellers. Eventually everybody in the barn passed out, including Talon. At one point, though, Megwadesk thought he had awakened from his stupor to see Old Molly crawling head first into the well, her green-and-black leather boots disappearing slowly as if gravity had no pull on her.

Megwadesk had rocked his head at such a strange sight, thinking, *No wonder these parties are always a smash. Man oh man, they sure sell some strong stuff here, eh!*

Then he had continued dozing.

Megwadesk wiped the mud off his soles on the edge of the porch steps, while Skoltch walked straight in. His hands hurt worst than ever now and he wondered if he could still hold a guitar chord. Working in the woods made his hands leathery and holding the axe all day often cramped his hands.

Chapter Four

The Second Coming

"I was just getting ready to check my net,"Skoltch hollered at Megwadesk, as they stamped the mud off their boots and hung their jackets, "when I heard you yelling! Gisúlk, Máli! I thought somebody was killing you! The way you were going on, I almost ran into the house to get my rifle! And then to find out it was just my dog – well, I didn't know who to throw into the ditch – the dog for playing with you or you for screaming like it was the end of the world! Nisgam nuduid, I'd hate to see you in a war! Here! Take a seat!"

"Boys oh boys, I'm telling you," Megwadesk replied, "if that bitch comes at me again, eh, I'm gonna slit it's throat from ear to ear! Cut it's damn head right off!"

Megwadesk kept his navy-blue cap on. He scratched his left arm through his shirt. It felt swollen but he could not tell for sure.

"How are you, anyway? Did it bite you anywhere?" Skoltch asked.

Megwadesk rolled up the sleeve and they looked at his arm. It didn't appear to be cut anywhere but it was swollen. Skoltch offered to bind it up but Megwadesk insisted that he was fine.

"Well at least have something to drink!" Skoltch said. "What will it be? Tea or coffee?"

"Tea, if you got some," Megwadesk replied.

"Sure we got tea, boy! We got bologna, too!" Skoltch bellowed. Megwadesk noticed a large scab on Skoltch's brow and he guessed rightly where it came from.

"You know what the Maliseets say about us, don't you? 'What's a Micmac breakfast? Tea and bologna!'"

Skoltch laughed at his joke as he struck a match and lit a kerosine lamp. Beside the lamp stood a jar of pickled babycorn. Megwadesk could hear Skoltch's wife snoring through the open bedroom door. Skoltch poured some water from a bucket into a kettle and set the kettle on the stove.

He put a cigarette in his mouth and added, "Say, you sure looked woebegone checking your net a few days ago! Your jaw just about dropped to the water! Whoa, there! I almost told my son to reach over with a bucket to catch your jaw before you lost it in the water! But you caught it in time! Nisgam nuduid! You had your empty net pulled out of the river and up over your head and you kept looking this way and that, and up and down, and shaking your head, and staring! Ho! I told my son, 'Get your handkerchief out because he's going to start bawling any minute now!' Ho, boy, you sure were a sight!"

That's Skoltch all right, Megwadesk noted. *He gets a little lucky 'n' he loses no time 'tall getting up there on his high horse 'n' he forgets how to talk to people in a sensible way! He's got to shout at the top of his lungs, eh, like he's talking to his lessers 'n' he's got to exaggerate everything, too, eh!*

"Since then, though, I haven't seen you check your net!" Skoltch shouted as he stood by the counter, his arms crossed over his chest. It seemed he forgot the cigarette. The tip of it constantly bobbed up and down as he spoke. "Is this your seventh day, or what? You've made the world and you've set the lamps in the sky, right, and now it's time to rest, huh! Ah, ha, ha! Or is your girlfriend keeping you in bed? What is it? Too much of that and you'll soon start to waste away! You won't want to do anything else! That's what my father told me! Gisúlk, Nisgam, he should have knowed! He got ten kids out of my Mum alone! That's before he took off to Cape Breton to start another brood! And, you know, come to think of it, that old geezer must have been right! He never did do much else! I had to learn fishing from my uncle! That's where my son is now – with my uncle. They went out to the breakwaters yesterday to spear eels! I miss my boy already! Anyway, he'll learn from the best – he'll be learning from Uncle Noel! Like I said, Dad could talk fishing but I never seen him so much as bait a hook or haul a minnow! So don't tell me your new little lady is getting you to be like he was!"

Whoa, there, big fella! Ho!"

Skoltch had acquired his nickname, which meant frog, because of his double chin. It was so enormous it seemed pendulous. The great width of his mouth and the thin, flat lips that lined it further enhanced his resemblance to a frog. The size of his mouth had never pleased Skoltch. In his youth he had spent many hours before the looking glass puckering his lips, trying to make his mouth smaller. Years later, he hit upon the idea of letting his facial hair grow to cover up his mouth but there must have been only a thimbleful of French blood in him. His beard was sparse.

"I should say it's your woman who's keeping you in bed," Megwadesk replied. "You don't see me check my net, eh, 'cause you don't get up early 'nough no more."

And Megwadesk slyly winked and quickly pointed by jutting out his bottom lip to Skoltch's bedroom door. Skoltch's wife kept snoring. Skoltch laughed heartily. Any comment ascribing virility to him, easily flattered him. Between hoots of laughter, Skoltch blushed and cried, "Nooo!" in a faint attempt to put the matter into sober perspective. At length, Skoltch regained composure.

"Nugú!" Skoltch announced, his face red. "Let's not talk about our better halves no more, huh!"

"Oh, come on." Megwadesk pretended disappointment.

"No, no, no! We'll save those stories for when we're out of ear shot! You're an eager young buck and all that, I know, so there are things you want to learn from an old nabéw like me! Ho, I can tell you stuff! But in due time, boy! In due time!"

Skoltch took a match out of the matchbox, struck it, and lit his cigarette. He inhaled peacefully. Skoltch's compressed eyes gleamed and dimples formed in his fleshy round face as he stood looking at the stove, impatient to hear another protest – another, "Oh, come on," – certain that Megwadesk had not taken his injunction to heart. Skoltch was reluctant to leave so soon, the laudable subject of his manly ardour, but he had felt it was only proper to show some degree of modesty, which was why he had feigned insistence on waiving the matter. Now he stood grinning at the steaming kettle, a suitable epic about his virility set to course from his mouth, just waiting for another protest and a chance to roar with bogus reluctance, "Well, all right! If you insist! I'll tell you a little something I know about women!"

Megwadesk, however, missed his chance to humour Skoltch. He shrugged his shoulders and said, "Whatever you say."

Skoltch found something suspect in this sudden indifference. To make matters worse, Megwadesk made Skoltch positively hostile by pointing out the sizable scab over his left brow and asking, "Is that cut on your head from a rock, eh? Are they still throwing rocks from the bridge?"

"Do you really care to know?" Skoltch growled. Then he sucked on his cigarette three times.

Megwadesk was taken aback, after a long pause, Megwadesk said, hoping to break the hostile silence, "I heard you're going to get a new sail-boat."

Skoltch ignored the question and said, "Well, if you really want to know, I did get hit with a rock! Now what do you want?"

"What do you mean?" Megwadesk asked. He thought Skoltch was asking him what he wanted that information for but that made no sense.

"What do you want? Why are you here?"

"Oh, that! I'm here to find out what's been going on at the bridge, eh. I haven't gone past it 'tall in six days now."

"Humph! Don't look like you'll be going past it any time soon either, so why are you worried?"

"I'm thinking of going to ykdánug, spearing eels, eh. Ain't had no luck 'tall this far upriver for too many days."

"Spearing eels, eh! I should head out there one of these nights, too, just to do some spearing with my boy! Nisgam! Kids sure grow up fast, eh?"

Skoltch didn't expect an answer. He was still feeling surly. He took a deep drag from his cigarette and then he said, "Yeah, I'm looking at a twenty-footer with a twenty-four foot mast!"

"A twenty-footer!" Megwadesk said, with the proper measure of wonder in his inflection. "Man oh man, that'll hold quite a load, eh, an' with a good breeze them wardens'll never catch you 'tall!"

Nobody owned a twenty-feet long boat in Messkíg. Sixteen-foot sail-boats, mostly scows equipped with centre-

boards, were standard. Still, Megwadesk was not spontaneously expressing his surprise for he had already heard about
the details of Skoltch's proposed purchase some time ago.
Skoltch, however, found his visitor's calculated response
flattering. "It's lapped hardwood!" Skoltch said. "It's a fancy
sloop, a real cutter, complete with a jib and a centre-board
as deep as I am tall! I can set three nets if I want to! It'll
easily hold that much catch! A twenty-foot cutter with high
gunwales! Nisgam! That's a lot of space!"

"Man oh man, that'll be a wonder," agreed Megwadesk.

Skoltch smiled indulgently and then, for the sake of modesty, he redirected the conversation again, deciding it was
time to offer some friendly advice.

"Well, anyway," he said, "if you're going to ykdánug just
make sure to go past the bridge by night, if you wanna avoid
trouble! Even a mere stub of a mast'll slip you by fast enough!
But then you have to hope the wardens don't see you, either! Jumping Moses, it's like we're a bunch of criminals,
eh! It's like we're the newcomers instead, huh! Can't touch
the animals! Can't touch the fish! Nisgam! We can't even
touch the trees! You see a good stand of ash, perfect for axe-
handles, and you go take a couple down – one or two, that's
all – and some milky-eyed madman's gonna run out with
his rifle and tell you to get away from his trees! Everything's
their's now! Gisúlk, Máli!

"Pretty soon they'll be telling us we can't keep time by
the moon 'cause that's gonna to be their's, too! You know
what really gets me, though, is how they point the finger at
us when the fish stocks go down! Isn't that something, huh?
They've had them great big boats fishing off the Grand Banks
and shipping millions and millions of tons out to every corner of the world since before the time of Christopher
Columbus! When they blame us, it sounds like this to me:
like one kid, who has taken and eaten most of the cookies in
the cookie jar, blaming a smaller kid for eating all the cookies just because that smaller kid took one cookie, which so
happened to be the last one! See? For thousands of years
we've been taking that one cookie every year, but when all
that's left is our one cookie and we still take it like usual,
well, we get called gluttons! And a lot worse things, too!
Anyway, it's boiling! You like your tea strong?"

"Éq! Black as a crow's butt, eh," Megwadesk answered.

"Six tea bags, then! I like mine strong too! One, two, three, four, five, six, and pick up sticks! Or, for around here, pick up switches! There we go! Hey, look at that!"

Megwadesk looked out the window above the counter. Hazy sunlight filtered through the clouds.

"You can stop shaking in your boots now, boy, 'cause it looks like it's gonna clear, after all!" Skoltch roared, as if Megwadesk had fled like a child to the security of Skoltch's house in fear of the storm.

"I didn't even notice 'tall that the thundering had stopped, eh," Megwadesk said.

"Oh, I know you didn't! But I did! I noticed right away – as soon as that last rod of lightning flashed four miles away! Nadóq, I said to myself, it's over now – that last one sounded like no more than a fart! It's over all right! I'll set the tea pot right here on the table!"

As he put the teapot down, there followed a faint flash and, several seconds later, another distant rumble.

"Humph!" was all Skoltch voiced. He took the butt out of his mouth and squashed it in a clay ashtray and he turned to the cabinets.

While Skoltch thrust his meaty arms into the cabinets to retrieve two cups and two saucers, a bowl of sugar, and a bag of home-made doughnuts, Megwadesk thought about the storm. Storms, especially very windy ones, used to be explained by his people as the doings of Wejúsyn, a giant bird, whose great beating wings moved the air. This, in turn, made him think again about the man in white and about spirit stories. Spirits, as far as he was concerned, were nothing more than tricks of nature, tricks that people misunderstood.

He had been mulling over this idea for several weeks but he could not share it with anyone. It was still too fuzzy in his head. He felt he had to bring together many examples before he could say clearly what it was he meant. And he knew that to talk about any idea before it had fully matured in his head was the worst thing to do, because people wouldn't understand it and they would only muddy up the water some more. Besides, Mimi often got impatient with his speculations. Megwadesk had learned that, with most people, it was best to skirt around an idea first just to see how they felt about things by slightly touching on the question.

Megwadesk thought about how he enjoyed talking to Mr. Severman because the preacher enjoyed talking about things that most people considered foolish, strange or dangerous. During their talks once, Megwadesk had told Mr. Severman that maybe what people sometimes called goodness was just the outcome of weakness and, to his surprise, the preacher had answered, "William Blake, the prophet-poet of England, would have agreed with you, my friend. He wrote that people who bridle their desires can do so because their appetites are naturally small to begin with. No virtue in temperance from that perspective – is there?"

Skoltch set the cups and saucers, and the sugar and doughnuts, on the table. Then he opened a drawer and took out two spoons and set those on the table as well.

"Help yourself!" Skoltch ordered. "I don't put up with timidity in my house! Go on, boy! I'm not serving anyone! If you can't fend for yourself, you'll starve – that's all!"

"Thank you," Megwadesk answered, as he poured the tea into his cup. He drank it black.

"Oquetédud! This is a man's tea, eh, a Micmac's tea, all right!"

"Oh, yes!" Skoltch answered and he sat and poured himself a cup, too, adding three heaping spoons of sugar.

The two men quietly sipped their tea for several minutes.

Skoltch pushed the doughnuts to his guest and said, "Here! Try some! They're good!"

Megwadesk took a doughnut and swallowed a bite and then washed it down with tea. Skoltch dipped his doughnut into his tea and then chewed on it. Megwadesk noticed the rain had stopped. He looked out the window to the east and saw a pair of rainbows, one fainter than the other. The rainbows reminded him of a promise of some kind – he couldn't remember exactly what it had been about – a promise anyway – that God had made to Noah after the flood.

Suddenly Megwadesk asked, "Do you believe in that Bible stuff, eh? You know, all the miracles like Jesus raising the dead?"

41

"Sure, I believe in Jesus," Skoltch answered, not at all surprised by the question. He had been expecting something like this from Megwadesk. For such an uncanny fisherman, Skoltch thought, Megwadesk still asked the foolish questions of a youth.

"Can you believe in a god who'll make everybody rise stark naked 'n' all rotted on judgement day, eh?" Megwadesk continued. The growing sunlight made him bold. He could voice his secret horrors now.

"Sure, sure," Skoltch answered with forged impatience. He was pleased actually, for this opportunity to wax philosophical. A conversation with Megwadesk was always good for that. "But you shouldn't worry about them details! Let the white people worry about all that stuff! Nisgam gejidoq! We didn't have nothing to do with his murder! As far as I see it, on judgement day Jesus will come down on a cloud and he'll go to all the reserves first and tell all the Indians to just keep right on fishing, that's all! Then he'll get back on his cloud again and fly off to Trenton and go deal with the white people there, and everywhere else there's whites – and, by God, they'll pay for killing him all right, and for killing all the land and all the rivers and all the fish and leaving none for us! Amudj! They'll pay! Jesus was a fisherman! And don't you forget it! He knew where to set his nets, too – even better than you, I'm sure! He understands us! So don't you worry!"

Skoltch's comments annoyed Megwadesk. He told Skoltch, "You make Jesus sound like Glúskeb almost, eh, the way he'll help us and all."

"Well, they're cousins, I think," Skoltch declared. "Or maybe step-brothers! I forget right now how it was my dad put it! My dad was only good for stories, you know! But anyway, Glúskeb took care of us for a long time till he got tired, 'cause we were always making trouble for him, going to war with all kinds of tribes and everything like that! Gisúlk, Máli! So Glúskeb needed a rest! Before he left, he called his cousin, Jesus, and told him to come on over and take care of us for a while! Sort of like babysit, I guess! So Jesus said, no problem, jínym! Remember, Malsum still had to be watched or else that devil would take over the world again! So Glúskeb knew somebody like Jesus had to be here while he went out west to sleep a bit!

"But Jesus was kinda lazy, see! He liked his wine too much, I think! Anyway, he stayed home and only sent his messengers to look after us! That's the priests and stuff! But you know how messengers are! Glúskeb never could leave anything up to his messengers, loon and rabbit! Nisgam gejidoq! If he did, they would make a mess of things! Éq! Bana total mess! So it's the same with these messengers from Jesus! Instead of just taking care of us and baptizing us and giving us decent burials, these priests turned around and invited all kinds of other people with them, see! Bana foolishness!

"So judgement day's going to come around just after Glúskeb wakes up and just before he gets back here! Glúskeb is going to shoot his arrow ahead of him and it'll land in the Minas Basin, see, to tell Jesus he can pack up his stuff and get ready to go back to his home! And Jesus'll get scared, see, 'cause he's let his messengers make a big mess of things here, and it's really all his fault 'cause he's been so lazy, see! Gisúlk, éq! That's when he'll come around on his cloud and tell us to keep right on fishing and then he'll take all the other people together, even the dead ones – he'll call them right up from their Loyalist graves and all – and tell them, 'Listen here,' Jesus will say, 'either you go back with me or you go to hell!'

"Of course, you know how stubborn white people are! Many of 'em'll stand around their farms with their shotguns in their hands! Nisgam! They'll be just ready to kill Jesus all over again, if he so much as steps near their potato gardens! So poor Jesus'll have no choice but to send Satan after them! Satan'll come out of the water with his red cape and red whip and flog the laggards! Some clever ones'll manage to run away and hide in the swamps, though! Then Glúskeb'll come back and if there's any left over – shotgun or not – he'll take them by the scruff of their necks and throw them across the ocean, and tell them to stay there! They can hide from Jesus and Satan but they won't be able to hide from Glúskeb, that's for sure!"

Megwadesk did not find the story helpful. In his mind, either one believed in the old ways or one believed in the white man's Christian ways and yet there were many sto-

✓ ries around which were a blend of the two.

"I've heard stories where Glúskeb and Jesus had contests and Glúskeb always won, eh," Megwadesk said. "First time I heard this one, though."

"Oh, yeah, Glúskeb always wins!" Skoltch said very seriously. "Dad told me them stories, too! Oh, there's hundreds of them! One time, some white guy came around here and wrote a couple down, but the old timers pulled his leg! Instead of telling him all the Glúskeb stories, they told him fairy tales, with Indians in them though, just to see if he'd write those down, too, and call them legends! Nisgam! And he did! So that's how much some people know! Ho! We're always pulling people's legs – and looking pretty serious when we're at it, too! But, anyway, about this Jesus and stuff! Meantime we got to go to church and all that just like a kid has to listen to a baby-sitter! But don't worry about all that judgement day stuff! It's just for white people really! That's why the priests are always going on about it, because they're guilty and they know it and it's always on their minds, bugging them like! So they go on and on about it! Me and you, we're okay and we'll keep right on fishing, either way! Personally, I wouldn't blink an eye if judgement day happened this afternoon!"

Skoltch coughed and then fell silent. His voice was hoarse from all the shouting. Talking down to people was exhausting sometimes.

"Oh, I'm not scared of that stuff, either. Don't get me wrong, eh," said Megwadesk. "I'm just curious 'bout what you think, that's all. But you don't really believe that silly story, eh? That's the matter with our people!"

"What's the matter? What're you talking about? Don't you know a good story when you hear one?"

"Too many of our stories are like that, that's all."

"Like what?"

"They're just like wishes that we keep holding tight to, eh, an' after a while alls we got's is wishes."

"What do you mean, 'wishes'? I'm telling you what my elders told me! It's like a story the prophets tell! It talks about what's gonna happen one day!"

"An' I say instead of wishing the white people'll just disappear one day and we'll all live happily ever after, we gotta

44

start dealing with the facts, eh. Geez, we keep acting like we
can just go on ignoring the real world, like we don't have to
change someday 'n' start picking up ways of surviving in
the white world!"

"That's not – "

"Sure it is! Sure, that's what it's about! Boys oh boys, just
look at the story they tell about Old Set-Ból coming back to
haunt the priest. They just wish the old priest could be scared
by something the way he can scare the people, eh, so they
make this story up 'n' it makes 'em feel good – like it really
happened. That's like justice for them. But, really, eh, it's
just a fill-in for justice. It's all really 'bout wishful thinking,
and nothing 'tall else! Nisgam nuduid, why do you think
people believe in spirits and witches for, eh? It's 'cause they
feel like they got no real power. So they need this magic
power. If they can't get back at the whites for stealing all the
land, then they'll say that the spirits like Jesus or Glúskeb or
whatever'll get back at them one day! That's no different
than anything else, either! If you do something wrong to
another fellow in Messkíg, 'n' you get away with it, like you
don't pay a fine or go to jail or nothing, eh, then that fellow'll
tell himself, *Well, maybe I can't do nothing but the spirits'll get
'im back 'cause what goes 'round comes 'round.* Then he'll feel a
little better. See what I mean? All these stories 'bout spirits
'n' medicine 'n' stuff is just a way of keeping our blinders
on! We don't even see half – "

"So that's all you see in them stories, huh?" Skoltch cut
in. "Then it's you who don't even see half of what them
stories are for! First off, let me tell you that I don't act like I
don't have to deal with the white world! I have to deal with
them people all the time and some of them are real nice but
lots of times they get away with things like throwing rocks
at people and stealing land left and right! Okay, then! This
story I told you tells me that we're not like them! We never
went across the ocean and stole their land and told them
they couldn't do this or they couldn't do that! So who's right?
We're right! Now if we're right, does it mean that we should
forget about our honest ways just because we're in a weaker
position now? No, sir! I don't think so! Like I said in the
story, we keep right on fishing and living the way God wants
us to! We don't just turn around and be like them, stealing

land, hurting people, taking kids away from their parents, breaking up families, destroying all the trees, being greedy, greedy, greedy! If they're right, then I'd rather be wrong! You see now what you missed in that story?"

"Well, let me put it 'nother way – " Megwadesk said but just then, the door opened and a brutal-looking middle-aged man with a twisted nose, a chipped eyebrow and a lopsided grin swaggered in. His hair was dishevelled and there were branches stuck to his clothing in a manner that hunters sometimes wore to camouflage themselves in the woods.

"Here to see godmother Molly!" the fellow demanded, banging the door shut behind him. Megwadesk glared at him. Even from seeing only his back, he knew it was Rancid.

Chapter Five

A Basket Full of Peril

There was a history of conflict between Rancid and Megwadesk. An overall bitter impression, rather than a chronological series of memories, regarding their past, always darkened Megwadesk's mind when he came face to face with Rancid. This bitter impression, however, could only be made sense of when unravelled event by event.

Rancid humiliated Megwadesk when Megwadesk was a boy. Rancid was then married with three children. Still, he often fooled around with any woman who cared to party with him and he frequently gave his wife vicious beatings. Megwadesk's father, a firm believer in the Catholic Church and a powerfully-built man with strong opinions, made enemies by preaching against bootleggers, drunkards, loafers and wife-abusers. Rancid had been man-handled and severely upbraided once by Megwadesk's father for abusing his wife so, for revenge, Rancid decided to make a show of his violence in front of Megwadesk.

One day, when he was twelve years old, as he was returning home from a baseball game, Megwadesk seen Rancid and his wife walking towards him. Rancid ordered his wife to stop and then he slapped the back of his wife's head with all his might, making her stagger forward as her hair flew. Megwadesk remembered stopping, stunned.

When she cried out, "What's wrong?" Rancid followed up with a punch to her right eye.

Then Rancid glared at Megwadesk and asked him, "Hell you looking at? Don't like what you see? Wanna do something 'bout it? Gonna run home and tell your daddy, maybe? Go 'head. Run home and tell daddy!"

Megwadesk said not a word. Nor did he tell anyone about the incident. Four years later, when Megwadesk was sixteen, he had his revenge.

It had been several months since he sprouted to his man size. He felt gangly and unsure. There was a dance. It was during St. Anne's Day celebrations. Megwadesk was in the audience. His group, which included two older cousins, had just concluded their show when Mimi went on stage. That had been the first time Megwadesk heard Mimi play. It became, however, impossible for Megwadesk to pay any more attention to her fiddle playing. Rancid started hollering at the top of his lungs, whirling and staggering in a crazy dance, all arms and feet, whooping and stomping and spilling his drink on the audience closest to the bandstand. Even the people on the dance floor next to the bandstand stopped to look at him.

Rancid's commotion irritated Megwadesk but he had been careful to keep his mouth shut. Although Megwadesk no longer had a boy's physique, he still felt his strength to be that of a boy. Megwadesk also knew that Rancid was not nearly as drunk as he appeared to be. He was aware that one of Rancid's favourite tricks was to appear helplessly drunk before starting trouble and when somebody challenged him, Rancid came alive, suckering the opponent on the nose. He also knew that Rancid never strayed too far from his friends.

Megwadesk was about to leave the dance, when Rancid, eyes glazed and eyelids droopy, lunged his way, splattering his clothes with a spray from a quart of beer. Megwadesk cursed and glared at Rancid. He had not intended to out-stare Rancid. He just wanted to give him a disdainful glance and walk off, but Rancid's eyes suddenly became extremely eager and seemed to hold his stare. Rancid straightened up.

"What's your beef, child?" he asked Megwadesk. "You kids these days think you're so damn hot!" Then he derisively spat out, "Children," and glanced up at the stage, adding, "yeah, heh, just a bunch of stupid children! Even bastards these days think they're too good for the rest of us!"

It seemed to Megwadesk, that Rancid had rated Megwadesk so contemptible that Rancid abandoned his drunken routine altogether. Rancid swaggered up to his face.

"Just 'cause people say you know where there's fish, think you're special or something? Humph! Like my godmother says, you Ligasudi kids act always like you're best at everything! If you're so damn good at fishing, should change your name maybe to Megwadesk Mudsucker 'stead of Megwadesk Ligasudi, huh!"

Rancid's buddies laughed. Megwadesk still hoped to get away without a fight. He never imagined his fishing skills inspired envy in anyone. Rancid's face was vivid. Megwadesk saw the black pores on his thick, twisted nose and on the bare spot of his chipped eyebrow. Then Rancid shoved his shoulder with the hand that held the bottle, and Megwadesk knew then that there would be no getting away from a fight.

Megwadesk was terrified. It was this fear, for his personal safety, that packed a furious spring into his muscles. Rancid didn't expect the attack. Rancid's hand, with the beer bottle, was still most detrimentally outstretched to his opponent's shoulder, leaving open his entire front. Megwadesk spiked his sternum with a jab. After delivering the first fury of blows, fear left Megwadesk and the thrill of the challenge took over.

Talon often prodded Megwadesk to sparring. He knew that he had learned some boxing skills but, next to Talon, Megwadesk never dared to appraise himself high at all. That night, however, he learned just how useful Talon's lessons had been.

Rancid doubled-over. Even as Rancid dropped to the ground, Megwadesk charged again with a series of rabbit punches to the back of Rancid's head and neck. Rancid was out for the rest of the fight but that still left three of his friends for Megwadesk to contend with.

While Rancid's friends stood around, momentarily stunned, Megwadesk's better judgement returned and he decided to run for it. As he bolted around the crowd, a powerful hand grabbed his elbow.

"Four of them!" Megwadesk thought, despair and panic sickening him. Megwadesk spun around and struck, but his blow was handily blocked.

"Let's give them what they want," Talon told him.

In the fight that ensued, Megwadesk's hands were full with one fellow while Talon rocked his first target – a huge man – with a tremendous hook to the jaw, leaping at him from his blind side, for the man had a puffy left eye already from a previous fight. Megwadesk thought, *Everybody who heard that punch must think for sure the giant's jaw's busted.*

Talon was about to follow with a left upper-cut to the big man's chin, when a kick to his hip threw him off balance. The husky fellow who kicked him, knew better than to try to out-box Talon. He made a dive to Talon's waist, knocking him to the ground, and began wrestling him. For a split second, Talon tried to push himself up by using his hands and his opponent lost no time in snapping a deadly choke-hold on him.

By then, Megwadesk's lips were bloody, but his antagonist was missing some teeth. Megwadesk heard Talon grunting and viciously kicking up the dust, his back stiffly arched, as if his only hope remained in trying to squash his tenacious adversary against the earth. Megwadesk knew he had to help him fast for Talon was choking so Megwadesk kicked his foe in the groin. The guy staggered back. Megwadesk kicked him in the testicles a second time just for good measure. This time the guy caught his foot and Megwadesk went down. Fortunately for him, Megwadesk's kick to the groin caught up to him and he quietly eased to a kneeling position. Megwadesk ran over to help Talon. He kicked all the wind out of the wrestler by planting a heavy boot on his back. The wrestler didn't let go fast enough for Megwadesk's satisfaction so, seizing the man by his hair, Megwadesk yanked back his trunk.

Meanwhile, the giant regained some composure, felt his jaw, shook his head ever so slightly, and then calmly walked away, not even glancing at the combatants. Megwadesk hopped around in uncontrollable excitement, expecting more enemies to rush them, while Talon spent his vengeance on the wrestler. Talon pinned the wrestler and then pounded his face. He knocked him out cold with the first two blows but in his blind fury – for he said later it had seemed to him that he had come very close to being choked to death – Talon kept hitting the hated face. Megwadesk hopped from Rancid to the guy with the aching testicles and back to Rancid again, ready to deal another blow if either made a move to get up. Suddenly Megwadesk realized it was over. He ran to Talon and dragged him off the unconscious fellow.

Megwadesk glanced at Rancid curled up on the ground and he thought, *Nope, he won't beat his wife in front of me again, eh.*

The dance continued without incident. That was the first time Megwadesk felt the strange and novel power that went with his new man frame. When Mimi finished playing, she walked over to where Megwadesk stood and asked him if he would be interested in accompanying her on the guitar the next time she played. They went for a stroll and Mimi told him that Rancid had tried to go out with her. She had spurned him, which was why he acted up when she went on stage to play. And then Mimi thanked Megwadesk for having intervened. That was their first date.

For a long time afterwards, it was rumoured that Rancid wanted a rematch – because he had been "suckered" he said – but Megwadesk eventually noticed that Rancid never stayed around too long in the same place where the two of them happened by.

Now Rancid turned around, after loudly shutting the door behind him, and said, upon seeing Megwadesk seated by the table, "Oh! See you got a visitor! Should come back later, maybe?"

"No, no. Have a seat!" Skoltch roared.

"Nope – have to go," Rancid answered and instantly he turned to leave but Megwadesk stopped him.

"Hold it, there – what's that 'round your neck?" Megwadesk asked him. "That looks like my pipe, eh? Is that my pipe hanging from your neck?"

There was a string of sinew going around Rancid's neck. It looked like a rosary but instead of having beads strung to it the string had the red berries of thorn bushes strung to it and where there should have been the crucifix was a small stone pipe.

"How should I know? Found it," Rancid answered. "liked it, sos I kept it!"

"Yes, that's my pipe all right! Where did you find it?" Megwadesk demanded, getting up from his seat. "Give it back here! What're you doing with my pipe hanging from a string like that, anyway, eh?"

"Hold it, boys!" Skoltch said, putting himself between the two men. "I know you fellas have had your scraps but that's a long time ago! Let bygones be bygones! Don't need to get all worked up about a little thing like a pipe now! Sit down, Megwadesk. And you, Rancid, if you found that pipe, then it belongs to somebody else! Come to think of it, that does look like the pipe I've seen Megwadesk smoking now and then when he's fishing. Where did you find it?"

"Found it on the shore. Was walking down by the river here a few days ago," Rancid replied, crossing his arms over his chest, "when I seen it in the water. Sos I took it. Mine now."

"You better give it to Megwadesk," Skoltch told Rancid. "It's his. I recognize it. He probably lost it while fishing."

"If you don't take it off your neck," Megwadesk added, "I'll cut it off your neck with my knife!"

Megwadesk noticed that small, white squares were painted on the stalks of the branches that were tied to Rancid's clothing. *What's that 'bout, I wonder,* Megwadesk thought. Rancid scowled for a moment, then he untied the pipe from the string of sinew and thorn berries. He handed over the pipe to Skoltch and then left the house without saying a word.

Skoltch returned Megwadesk his pipe. Then, turning around to seize the teapot, he said, "I'm gonna pour me another cup. How about you, you want another cup!"

"Sure, thanks," answered Megwadesk, taking his seat again. Both of them felt embarrassed about the incident with Rancid. Megwadesk was embarrassed at the way he had behaved. He wondered if Skoltch thought him to be petty in holding a grudge for so long. Skoltch was embarrassed for his mother's godchild, Rancid, who had lost face again.

After Skoltch was seated, Megwadesk said, "I haven't been catching a thing here, eh. Mimi 'n' I are out of food now. I'm not worried 'bout myself, see. Nisgam! If I was just by myself, well, I'd head out to the breakwaters today 'n' I'd survive, eh. No problem 'tall. But I gotta think 'bout my little lady, see."

Skoltch listened and squirmed in his seat. He knew he could not refuse to help Megwadesk, from whom he had borrowed in the past, but he found it terribly inconvenient to be bothered with financial matters at this time. It never failed to happen this way. Just when he had enough money saved to buy the thing he had his heart set on – in this case, the elegant cutter he had mentioned to Megwadesk – somebody had to come along and ask for a portion of his capital. He hoped Megwadesk would ask for food only. He had plenty of that to spare. Skoltch set the cup down on the table and crossed his arms over his chest, resting them over his huge gut. As he listened to Megwadesk, he scratched his right elbow, and turned his head to look out the window. The sun was burning with a vengeance. Motes caught in the sunbeams from the window floated over the counter, rising and falling in chaos. "You know, Skoltch, outside me and her, you're the first one to hear this, eh," Megwadesk continued. "Well, that's why I'm coming to you really, 'cause I know she can count on you, eh. 'Specially in these times. She's pregnant, you know."

Skoltch raised his sparse eyebrows and looked at Megwadesk, whose eyes, because of the dark tinges around them, looked especially solemn when he was serious. It was a tradition in Skoltch's family for the father to notify the man, whom he wanted to be the godfather to his child, of the pregnancy before letting other men know. Megwadesk surprised Skoltch, but the surprise was a pleasant and flattering one. Skoltch assumed he was being asked to be the child's godfather and this thrilled him. He immediately visualized the child as a boy and this image, in turn, brought a series of sporting adventures to his mind.

"Yep," said Megwadesk, "she's gonna have a baby, eh. An', well, she's gonna be eating for two people from now on."

Megwadesk nodded and took a sip of his tea.

"I guess this old nabéw doesn't have to teach you a thing, after all!" roared Skoltch, banging the top of the table with his right fist – then he laughed. Megwadesk coughed. He swallowed a mouthful of tea but it went up his nasal passages instead. Megwadesk bent down at the waist and kept coughing and Skoltch laughed even harder, thinking Megwadesk was laughing, rendered powerless by his witty remark.

"Ho! This nabéw doesn't have to teach you a thing, after all, aye!" Skoltch repeated, his sparkling eyes pressed into curved slits by his cheeks. Megwadesk kept coughing and hacking. Skoltch leaned over towards him to pat his back. Megwadesk's cap fell off. Skoltch blushed and hooted and said, "Nooo! Enough!" Then he laughed some more.

Megwadesk snatched his cap off the floor and slipped away from Skoltch's friendly blows. He went to the counter, where he dipped an aluminum cup into the bucket of water and drank.

"Nugú!" Skoltch cried. "Let's not get on that subject again! Not until we're out of earshot!"

"Yes," said Megwadesk, and his voice squeaked.

This made Skoltch laugh again. When he was through hooting and laughing, Skoltch said, "My, my, my! So your little lady is going to have a baby! Well, well, well!"

Megwadesk replaced his cap on his head. He carefully swallowed another mouthful of water before he answered.

"Yes," he said, and this time his voice did not squeak, but it was not strong either.

"Well, why didn't you say so? And you want me to be the godfather, right? Hey! There's nothing I like better than giving candies to the little ones on New Year's Day!" Skoltch said, referring to the tradition of giving away treats and presents to one's godchildren on the first of every January.

Megwadesk didn't know what to say. He remembered too late it was a tradition in certain families for the father to announce his wife's pregnancy to the man he wished to be the godfather, before announcing it to any other man. He used to wonder why some people had the most unlikely godparents. Now the answer was apparent to him. Too many inexperienced fathers opened their mouths before thinking. For a second, Megwadesk thought he had the way out of his dilemma. He would tell Skoltch it was really too bad but he had already announced this news to another man, like his uncle or his brother. Then he remembered telling Skoltch nobody else knew about the pregnancy yet.

"Bunáne, guís!" Skoltch went on talking, miming a New Year's handshake. He faced the doorway and bent low from the waist while still seated, pretending to be shaking a toddler's chubby arm, wishing him a happy New Year. "Oh, yes! Godfather Skoltch never forgets! Here's your candies, son! And look what I got you! A rod!" Then he turned to Megwadesk and said, "See that? Did you see the present I gave him? A fishing rod! Nisgam nuduid! You don't have to worry! He'll get all kinds of attention from me! I've got only one other godchild, you know! And he's all grown up now! Me, I like the little ones! Oh boy!"

"I'm sure you'll make a good godfather," Megwadesk said slowly. "But, mm, wouldn't you, mm - "

"Here she is! Talking about little ones, here's my angel! Come here, Little Molly! Don't be afraid of the strange man! He's a friend of mine! Come on! Say good-morning to your father!"

A girl stood on the stairway, four steps from the top step. She had left open the bedroom door facing the top of the stairs. Sunlight burnished her brown hair, etching her head in a halo of gold. Upon seeing a stranger in the house, she had stopped her descent in mid-stride. She wore a long soft cotton shirt that served as a gown. Megwadesk thought she was no more than four years old. In her arms she cradled a hand carved doll.

The girl walked down the stairs and then skipped to where her father sat. Little Molly stared at Megwadesk with large eyes that Megwadesk feared would burst into tears any second. But to his delight Little Molly smiled and said, raising her doll, "This is Annie."

Two of Little Molly's front teeth were missing. Her smile made Megwadesk chuckle. Little Molly quickly cupped her mouth with one hand, remembering she had lost another tooth just recently. She covered her mouth and laughed and then walked to where Megwadesk sat and showed him the doll.

"See?" she said again. "That's Annie. She was singing."

The innocence of children always deeply touched Megwadesk, sometimes even to the point of distress. While innocence always delighted Megwadesk, he could never dispel the foreboding shadow of experience, with all its inevitable heartbreaks and cruelties, hovering over it. Then innocence seemed like an illusion and he could not fully participate in its joy. Megwadesk now wondered if Little Molly, while travelling with her parents on their boat, had already suffered the indignity of strangers throwing rocks at her and hollering vile words at her parents. He wondered if she had been on the boat when the rock tore into her father's forehead.

Little Molly set the hand-carved doll on his knee and asked him, "Did you hear her singing upstairs? She was singing for the sun to come out."

"No, I didn't," Megwadesk answered. "She must have been singing quietly."

"No-oo!" Little Molly said, shaking her head from side to side. And then she added, shrugging, "Well, kind of quiet, I guess. But the sun heard her! How come you didn't?"

"Molly, come here and quit bugging the man!" Skoltch said. "Were you asking me something?"

"No-oo! Maybe Annie."

"I didn't mean you," Skoltch said. "I'm asking Megwadesk."

"Oh! Mm, what was I . . . ? Oh! Yes. I was wondering 'bout that godfather business, mm, if you, well, you might want to, mm, think on it some more, eh."

Little Molly leaned her back on her father's knee, sticking out her stomach. She had her doll in a neck-hold in her right arm. She pointed with her free hand at Megwadesk and said, "He's always saying, 'mm,' aye, daddy?" Then she laughed, covering her mouth.

Megwadesk laughed out of embarrassment.

"What?" Skoltch shouted. "Think about it? Nonsense! Do you stop and think when you get a personal invite to a feast? Nisgam! Of course not! It'd be an insult to spurn such an invite! I'm honoured to be your son's godfather! Don't worry about it! You got my word!"

"Look, daddy," Little Molly said, having strolled to the screen door to look outside at the cloud of evaporation rising from the damp grass in the field. "It looks smoky outside like when you cooked last night."

Skoltch chuckled, glancing at Megwadesk, and said, "Don't exaggerate, sugar."

"Where's grammy?"

The little girl's question stopped Skoltch dead.

"Huh? Grammy?" Skoltch asked.

"Mm-hm. Where's Grammy Molly, dad? She wasn't in

her bed."

Little Molly was named after her grandmother, with whom she shared the same room.

Skoltch looked at Megwadesk and said, "Maybe you rightly guessed I was hesitating! See, well, I. . . . There's something I'm not sure of now, something I forgot, and I just remembered, and I don't know if it's allowable for me to do the honour! I mean, to be the godfather, and all! I don't know if I'll be allowed!"

Megwadesk felt relieved. "Sure," he said, "don't let it bother you."

"No, no! I'm sure you'd like to know why but I can't explain! I'll tell you another time! I will!"

"Daddy, where's Grammy Molly, I said!" Little Molly demanded, returning to lean on her father's leg. For some reason Megwadesk couldn't understand, Skoltch seemed embarrassed.

"Don't worry about your grammy," Skoltch told Little Molly, awkwardly patting her head. "She's working in the barn! She'll be back soon!"

Skoltch put another cigarette in his mouth, lit it, then looked at Megwadesk and said, "Listen, I better get going! I'll get back to you on that godfather business! Meantime, don't worry about your little lady! I've got enough food here! What do you need?"

Skoltch got up and opened the cellar door.

"I got salted mackerel, dried salmon, and dried moose meat. Then there's carrots in the bin; turnips, potatoes – well, you got those in your garden already! I got fiddleheads and my mother pickled some great babycorn, too! Oh, here's a jar of it right on the counter! Take it! I'll get some more from the cellar!"

Megwadesk took the jar of pickled corn and walked to where his jacket hung on a hook. He put his jacket on and slipped the jar into its left pocket while Skoltch continued talking.

"Tell you what, I'll just go down there and bring something of everything for now! Meanwhile you take as much flour as you need from that bag! There's a clean pail under the counter!"

"Can I go downstairs, too, daddy?"

"No, you stay up here! I'll be back in a second!"

Little Molly dropped her doll on the floor and ran to the counter, shouting, "I know where the pail is! I know where the pail is! I'll show you! I know!"

She swung open a counter door and yelled, "There it is! See? You want me to get it? I can crawl in there! You want to see me?"

Before Megwadesk could answer, Little Molly ducked under the counter. Megwadesk walked to the 100 lb. flour bag that stood in the corner and ploughed his hand through the top of it until he felt the handle of a dipper. Little Molly hopped out with the pail. She triumphantly handed it over to Megwadesk.

"I got it, see! See! Here it is!"

"You're a smart girl," said Megwadesk. "Listen, can you find me a clean towel, eh, so I can wipe the dust off the pail?"

"I know where it is!"

"Good."

"I'll bring it!"

"Okay."

"It's in the closet!"

"Bring it over."

Little Molly returned with a face towel. Megwadesk wiped the inside of the pail clean. Then he took the dipper and thrust it into the flour and dumped the dipperful of flour into the pail.

"One!" shouted Little Molly.

Megwadesk thrust the dipper into the flour and dumped it again into the pail.

"Two!" shouted Little Molly. "Five more to go!"

Megwadesk kept filling the pail with flour.

"Three! . . . Four! . . . Five! Two more to go! . . . Six! . . . And seven! Yeah!"

Skoltch laboured up the stairs with a basket of assorted food. On top were several small jars of pickled babycorn. He set the basket on the table. Megwadesk also set the pail of flour on the table.

"There's a frying-pan lid under the counter that'll fit over the pail!" Skoltch told Megwadesk.

"I'll get it!" Little Molly volunteered.

"No," said Skoltch. "You get me a large towel to put over

this basket!"

Little Molly dashed to the closet. Megwadesk leaned under the counter, found the lid, and then set it on the pail.

"I can't find any big towels!" Little Molly shouted.

"That'll be fine," Megwadesk told Skoltch. "I can take the basket as it is."

Megwadesk cradled the basket on his left forearm.

Skoltch wiped the sweat off his brow and asked, "So when's the wedding? I know Mimi doesn't care for our priest, so I'm guessing you'll be getting married in Weladeg instead – am I right?"

Most of Skoltch's cigarette was reduced to a stick of ash which remained firmly in one piece.

"We don't know yet, eh. We haven't decided."

"Well, you better decide quickly!"

Megwadesk grabbed the pail by the handle with his right hand. He was about to thank Skoltch, when he heard somebody entering the porch. He stepped to the side of the door to allow the door to swing open. When the door opened, Megwadesk was partially hidden behind it. An old woman stepped in. She did not notice Megwadesk.

"I've been doing your work all night again!" the old woman yelled at Skoltch. She held in her dark and bony left hand thorn shoots bound together by a black leather strap to form a switch. The thorn shoots were painted a brilliant crimson. She raised the glistening thorn lash to Skoltch's face and shook it. The arching stick of ash broke off from the butt of Skoltch's cigarette and crumbled over his belly.

Although Megwadesk recognized Old Molly, the incongruity of her condition baffled him. The old woman was soaked right through. Like most women in Messkíg, she wore several long skirts, one over the other. Her whole attire – all her red skirts, her red-and-green blouse, and her green-and-black leather boots – were dripping with water. This surprised Megwadesk, for not only had the rain stopped some time ago, but he was under the impression Old Molly had been working in the barn. This surprise did not compare to the astonishment of seeing her long greying hair, usually tied in a bun, hanging loose down to her waist and all lined with seaweed and thick green strands of river moss! The distinct briny pungency of stagnant inlet waters issued from her.

"If you worked half as hard as my godchild did, we would be wealthy by now!" she shrieked. "What are you still doing here, you lazy dolt? Watching you here, you'd think you were the Maker of Cain, on his day off! Go down to the river this instant! Your nets are loaded full! Go on! Your work is waiting for you!"

Skoltch backed away, thoroughly humiliated and appalled. Megwadesk noticed Skoltch kept angling his head towards him, to signal Old Molly and warn her there was somebody else in the house but the old woman did not catch the gesture. Megwadesk, uncomfortable in witnessing this private scenario, let his presence be known with a cough and a quick word of thanks to Skoltch.

"I'll leave now," he mumbled.

Old Molly wheeled around and drilled her vicious grey eyes into his ingenuous gaze. Her pale eyes were horrible in contrast to her dark and deeply wrinkled face. Only for an instant was her right eye open. Then it closed and remained shut. The right side of her face was twisted, constricted in knots of nerves and muscles that kept her right eye sealed.

Although she was at least a head shorter than Megwadesk, Old Molly seemed to stare down at him, her head tilted back and her lower jaw thrust out. She pulled her thin lips taut, baring her bottom teeth. Megwadesk found her blazing left eye so forceful that he felt like shielding his own. Old Molly was one of those very old people he was acquainted with only from a distance. Until then he had thought of her as a shy old woman who kept to herself. Her intensity took Megwadesk by complete surprise. Suddenly, Old Molly's left eye widened with fear. Again, for an instant, her right eye popped open.

"What is this?" she cried.

Megwadesk was so disconcerted he did not realize Old Molly was staring at the basket of food in his arm. He thought there was something hideous he was unconscious of in his appearance. For a moment he wondered if he had absentmindedly wiped his face with his floured hands and if this were why Old Molly was frightened, thinking she was looking at a ghost.

"What is this?" Old Molly cried again. But this time she

tossed her thorn switch aside and dashed towards Megwadesk and seized the basket of food from him. Her right eye closed again. In her anger Old Molly did not notice the pail with the frying-pan lid on it that Megwadesk held in his right hand. The basket overflowing with food took all her attention. She slammed the basket on the table and then stared at Skoltch.

"Don't you know anything?" she upbraided Skoltch, trembling with anger and shaking her head gravely.

Without waiting for his response, Old Molly faced Megwadesk again. This time she smiled, although her icy grey eye remained inhospitable. As she spoke, however, her eye changed and acquired all the loneliness of a misty day.

"Dear, I'm sorry for acting so rude," she said, "but I've suffered so much upset these past few days that I'm afraid my temper has got the worst of me. Please, you must excuse me, dear. You must forgive me. Normally I wouldn't begrudge any one of food. Nisgam nuduid! I believe in sharing and in working together. I believe we have to look out for each other. Otherwise how could we survive? Gisúlk! Look at us now! Each year we bury so many of our little grandchildren! How could we survive? No! We have to share! But, you must understand, dear, others depend on us, too. Our poor relations have put a strain on us and, as I've told my son over and over again, we can't help everybody. You try to help everybody and you end up doing nobody any good. You just run yourself down to nothing. And then where are you? Are you that much ahead? And who can count on you then? So I tell my son, help your in-laws and your brothers and sisters first. Everyone else has some relation they can go to. Isn't that right, dear? Amudj! That's how it goes. And I tell him, think about the old ones first. The young people have a good chance. They can fend for themselves. Isn't that so? When I was young, why, nobody ever saw me begging! There's nothing shameful about asking for help, mind you. It's just that I would have considered myself useless to count on begging! So, dear, even in my old age now, I always remember the helpless come first. But all this strain has put me in a very bad temper! Please, understand, dear."

Old Molly's wrinkled brow and the delicate folds under her eyes spoke years of anguish. Her long wet hair stuck to her face and droplets of salt water rolled down her trenched cheeks.

No matter how stirring Old Molly made her words, they did little to ease the humiliation Megwadesk felt. A resentment stirred deep in his heart at how he had just been treated. It was difficult enough for him to ask for help, but to receive help only to have it snatched back as though he had been deemed, on second thought, to be an untrustworthy man was an outrageous insult. He wanted to get out of the house as fast as he could. Old Molly's long-winded explanation only prolonged his great discomfort. It seemed like she would go on and on talking so Megwadesk cut in.

"I didn't realize you were having such hardship, eh," he said heatedly. He was completely flustered. He marched out the door, mumbling something to the effect that he was sorry for his thoughtlessness and now he had other things to attend to.

Skoltch raced after him and caught up to him outside the porch. The girl, Little Molly, also raced to the door to see what would happen. She heard her father apologize, and saw him hand some money to Megwadesk, who wouldn't take it. Then Skoltch stuffed the bills into Megwadesk's right jacket pocket and quickly walked back into the house.

Megwadesk stared at the door. For a minute he gazed at Little Molly as if she were a completely incomprehensible phenomenon. Finally, he decided to give the money back to Skoltch.

He walked up to the door, staring at the girl, and he heard the old woman inside the house yell, "How could you give him anything of mine? I grew that special corn! It's like my flesh! Don't you know better than to hand anything like this over to somebody I'm foiling? In the wrong hands, this is ammunition against me!" He turned around, and started down the driveway.

Chapter Six

Traplines Of The Mind

Megwadesk heard the dog growl its curses from its shelter under the porch but he didn't pay any attention to it. He walked in the shade of the jackpines down the curving driveway. A breeze stirred the boughs and sprinkled him with drops of water. Though it was very hot, the thick grass by the roadside was still matted down and drenched. In open spaces, clouds of evaporation hovered over the grass. Megwadesk found the weather strange. It should have been cool after the storm. The heat meant that this morning's storm had been a mere a prelude to a greater storm.

In the trees, spiders were busy stringing invisible strands between the branches. A filament tickled Megwadesk's face. He absently scratched his forehead with his left hand. His arm ached. When he reached the road, he looked down past the graveyard to the river. Yesterday morning the river had been sparkling but now the sunlight didn't penetrate the water. The sky reflected the dull glow of an old aluminum pot. The river was dirty. And it was very high.

"Can't get too upset about it," he muttered. "I don't have my eel-spear anyway."

With or without his spear, though, he had a strong and vengeful impulse to get on his boat and head out to the breakwaters, not to return until he had triumphantly reversed his luck. He imagined spearing an astounding number of eels and amazing all the fishermen of Messkíg. He and Talon would share the work. His father would welcome them back home. Nobody would ever insinuate he was a beggar again!

His head began to throb. Only if he could get one good

peaceful night of sleep! He looked to his right and saw the houses of Messkíg huddled as though in fear or for comfort – Megwadesk was not sure which and then thought that perhaps it was both – around the imposing white church and the smaller community hall. He looked to his left at the hill that hid his tiny home from view. He saw the wide road he had cleared running close to the top of it. The stacked logs and the brush piles were visible at regular intervals. He would work on the road again. After enough work he would shake off his headache and his sleepiness and he would, like a runner after reaching the point of exhaustion, suddenly get his second wind. The trick was to not allow himself to rest, not to let himself sleep and dream. When he dreamed, all he did was run and run in terror for what seemed like years. There was no rest in that.

The river looked dull and he noticed that the reflections of the woods shrank down to the tips of the foremost trees. He realized that this was because he was on high ground. The closer to the water he was, the deeper the reflections of the World-Below-the-Water became and the power of that inverted world grew stronger. But from the hilltop the grip of that submerged world weakened and the river mirrored the Sky-World instead.

As he walked down the road towards the cemetery, the sensation that something was amiss terribly troubled him. He wondered what was wrong with the picture. He felt something was missing but he dismissed this sensation merely as an aspect of his irritation.

Then he wondered why Old Molly had not taken the pail of flour from him. He wondered why she had told Skoltch, "I have been doing your work." Megwadesk thought perhaps Old Molly had been bootlegging in the barn. But then why was she soaked through with salt water? And what had she meant by "foiling"? He felt a shiver coming on and he tried to suppress it but his shoulders only jerked more violently when the shudder stubbornly surged up his spine.

His mother had once told a story about a witch who could hurt a person by using an object that belonged to the victim. This witch was vulnerable to the same sort of manipulation so she had to keep some of her precious belongings well guarded. Megwadesk grunted disgustedly. He scorned himself for making such foolish and fanciful connections.

If I could stop thinking this way, eh, he told himself, *then I'd be rid of an old weakness. Last night I fled when I was 'bout to take some bass from Skoltch's net. An' why? Only 'cause I was scared of witchery and retaliation! Pah! Am I any better off now for my stupidity? Not 'tall!*

He felt his pipe in his pocket and he could not help but recall what his mother had said concerning power and property. "One time," she had said, "Indians used to have power objects, things they seen in visions, you know, and these things, these power objects – deúmel they called 'em – they had to keep their deúmel under guard all the time, 'cause suppose somebody bad steal 'em, well, they can use 'em – these bad people can – to make people sick, to hurt 'em, even kill 'em. So nowadays people say there's no more power objects, so people got nothing to guard against. But that's not all true. Okay, it's true that not many people have power objects now – least not the kind you get from visions and fasting and stuff. But really, all a witch needs to get you with is something you handle all the time. Don't have to be a deúmel, you know. After a while, you handle something everyday, that thing is like a power object, too. It's not as strong, 'cause it's not from a vision, see, but it's still got you – your own power – all around it, see. That's why we believe a man's gotta keep such things as his spears, his axe, his knife, his pipe, his gun – all these things that his fingers are always wrapped around – he's got to keep 'em all safe. It's from your fingertips, see, that a good deal of your power comes out. But even today, you still got real power objects around, like the olden time kind. Even today! Yes, sometimes it's stones, sometimes it's switches, sometimes it's plants, sometimes it's seeds. Can be anything. In the olden times everyone had such an object. Everybody had a vision quest, that's why. But nowadays only the medicine people – or young people schooling on medicine – only them, they keep power objects like that. But like everything else in this world, some are good and some are bad. That's the way it is now."

Megwadesk thought, *Well, so what if Old Molly's a witch? And so what if she's trying something on me, eh? It's all what I told Skoltch – yes, it's all just wishes 'n' nothing else 'tall. We'll see what her silly wishes 'mount to when I clean their net of bass tonight! Real power is doing things and facing the real world!*

Then he thought about Skoltch and he felt a pang of conscience. *Maybe Skoltch's got nothing to do with any of Old Molly's business,* he thought. *But what business? I'm thinking like this whole witchery nonsense is for real, eh – like it's that stuff that's got my net so unlucky!*

Pain shot up his left forearm. His arm felt like it had been squeezed in a vice. He remembered hearing his jacket tear when the dog had pulled on its right sleeve so he reached under his right armpit with his aching left hand. He felt the rip in the back where the sleeve joined the body of the jacket.

He did not want to go back to his house. A pail of flour at the price of a torn jacket was a poor bargain to show for. He wondered if he was doomed to keep returning to this situation of embarrassment and incompetence? The sunlight pierced his eyes. Megwadesk recalled when he was eleven years old and his grandfather had hired him to tend a trapline.

His grandfather had done so well with the one trapline that he had been able to buy more traps to set another trapline. His grandfather told him he would be paid twenty percent of the value of the furs. Megwadesk understood this to mean he would be paid according to how much he caught. For a month he worked on the trapline. In that whole month, while his grandfather was busy skinning every night, Megwadesk trapped only three beavers. The contrast between how bountiful the trapline had been when his grandfather was working it and how unsuccessful it was when he, Megwadesk, was tending it became painful to him. At first he had attributed his bad luck to the weather but as weeks went by he became convinced that, despite his best efforts and his diligence, he had been somehow at fault. Finally, he told himself, either he was born to be a trapper or he wasn't.

What had pained him most was the belief he had disappointed his grandfather. When he couldn't stand it any longer, Megwadesk asked his grandfather to relieve him of his job. His grandfather tried to talk him out of quitting by telling him he should not be discouraged because it took a lifetime to be a good trapper. When Megwadesk insisted, his grandfather paid him an amount considerably more than the twenty percent his three beavers should have netted. When Megwadesk asked why he was getting so much, his grandfather answered, "Because this is your cut from what we made this month."

Megwadesk realized his grandfather meant twenty percent of the furs they had trapped *together*. Megwadesk could not return the money without insulting his grandfather. Years later, Megwadesk understood his grandfather had hoped the money would provide him with the incentive to keep trapping but, at the time when he received the money, Megwadesk had been overwhelmed by guilt and by an indelible impression of absolute unworthiness. This memory with its entire despair and self-loathing returned whenever Megwadesk experienced a humiliating setback.

With this memory stinging him, Megwadesk could not face the thought of going home with nothing more than just a pail of flour. There were other people he could visit but first he had to take the pail of flour home. One thing he swore not to do, however, was to ask help from his parents. His father, an ardent believer of the Catholic Church, after learning Megwadesk and Mimi planned to shack-up, shouted that Mimi had as much morality as a dog. He added, paraphrasing the Bible in a fervour of righteousness, that it would have been better off for her and for everybody in the community to have a millstone tied around her neck and then dumped into the river. To ask help from his parents after such an insult would feel a hundred-fold worse than when he took the money from his grandfather.

Megwadesk decided he would lie to Mimi. He would tell Mimi that Skoltch had promised him a share in the coming night's haul. The thought struck him as ingenious. It took care of two problems at once. First, it changed the outcome of his visit to Skoltch from a defeat to a triumph. Second, it saved him the problem of staging an elaborate show of heading out to spear eels. Ever since he promised Mimi he would go spearing eels, Megwadesk had been concerned about how he could fulfil his word when he did not even have his spear with him. After this ingenious lie Mimi would not expect him to spear eels when he had to work Skoltch's net.

"Even Glúskeb deceived people now and then," he said.

He took off his jacket, folded it and tucked it under his left arm. If he wished to sustain the illusion of a triumphant visit, then he could not allow Mimi to see the tear on his jacket.

When he reached the cemetery, he realized what it had been about the scene that had troubled him. The twenty-feet tall white wooden cross had been struck by lightning. It lay on the ground, the stem in shreds. Only a giant splintery stake remained upright.

Chapter Seven

An Exact Measure of Honey

When Megwadesk entered the house, he was relieved to find that Mimi was not there. He could hang his jacket up on the nail without worrying about her spotting the tear. He wondered where she had gone.

He set the pail of flour on the floor and he hung his cap and his jacket, with the inside facing out. There were no rips on the inside lining. He took the pail of flour again and set it on the little table by the window. He looked at the tiny moccasins and the little rattle hanging from the roofbeam. And then the entire house took on a different appearance.

Everywhere he turned he saw things he had not noticed before. The porcupine quill designs on the baskets were less intricate and more elegant in their simplicity. Soft yellows and blues dominated the designs. Springtime and fertility motifs, such as the eight-pointed flower and the green doubled-curves representing fiddleheads, circled the baskets in endless configurations. There was even a silhouette of a female moose and her young one on one basket.

Megwadesk walked to the sewing machine. In a basket beside the table were rags cut into small squares. Mimi was making a little quilt. Megwadesk lifted the square rags from the basket. In the bottom of the basket, where Mimi kept her yarn and darning needles, Megwadesk discovered a little yellow woollen hood. Beside it was a piece of lace that would eventually trim the hood. Megwadesk replaced the square rags inside the basket and straightened his back.

He looked at the linen shelf. He had wondered several times, just in passing, why Mimi had bought so many white towels. Now he walked to the shelf to take a closer look. He pulled out one white towel and grabbed one of its corners, snapping it in the air a couple of times to unfold it. The white towel turned out to be a diaper. He slowly folded the cloth diaper and returned it to the shelf. He chuckled. No wonder Mimi had teasingly called him a fool this morning. How had he missed all these indications?

He said, "Well, now it's my turn to add something here!"

He thought of how Mimi and he would be busy in the coming months. Not only did they have to prepare for the child but they had to prepare for a wedding as well. Megwadesk thought of how he had tried to convince Mimi that Father Colérique was a changed man, even when he really did not believe so. What troubled Megwadesk was the idea of converting to a new religion. He did not think it was so much a religious issue as it was a community issue. He was no longer a devout Catholic but it was hard for him to envision a life alienated from the community because of religion. Yet it was difficult, too, to imagine that a person with such winning ways about her as Mimi could be ostracised for any length of time. Before they had shacked-up, even his father had never tired of praising Mimi as the most enterprising young woman in Messkíg. He had also admired her ability to persuade people to her arguments.

Megwadesk walked to a large wooden trunk that served as his tool box. It was in the corner closest to the door. He took out an axe, a handsaw, a tin can of assorted nails (many of them bent, saved from old pieces of wood), a hammer, a whetstone, a drawknife, his sharpest crooked knife, a tin can filled with broken glass pieces, several sheets of sandpaper, a pencil and a ruler. He put these tools into a smaller tool box and walked outside with it. He went to the back of the house, where the extended roof kept the firewood dry.

The firewood was stacked up against the wall. Beside the firewood, kept above ground by blocks of old wood, were the planks and scrap lumber left over from the building supplies and on top of this lumber were his mast and boom with the canvas sail wrapped around them. The centreboard leaned against the woodpile. Overhead, on a rack right under the rafters, were various lengths of hardwood he had logged from the woods. It was mainly white ash and maple.

Although all the split hardwood was very straight, to be

resoaked and then carved into axe-handles later in the year, there were several naturally curved pieces, that were cut from arching branches. Megwadesk sculpted such curved pieces into exceptionally lightweight runners for the sleds he built and sold to loggers in the winter. In such pieces, he did not sacrifice resilience for lightness because the grain of the wood followed the shape of the intended design.

He selected a piece of bent maple from which he had already chopped off two runners. With the sides already chopped off, the width of the remaining strong grain was too narrow to provide another pair of runners. But it was just wide enough for small rockers. Megwadesk took the curved maple piece and walked towards the garden.

His happiness was incomplete on this special day. He missed his father, now more so than ever. It had been over three months since he had last talked to his father. And how, he wondered, would he feel when the child was born. He was still distant with his father? He knew his father could say the most outlandish things during his fits of indignation, things he would regret but could never apologize for, and yet Megwadesk did not know of another man whose company he found so delightful.

"Dad," Megwadesk suddenly asked aloud, "but isn't it written that a man will cleave to his wife?"

And so what that the priest don't bless us? he thought. *Mimi's still my wife.* He wished he could have talked to Talon. He would have felt better.

Megwadesk walked to the work table that stood between the potato garden and a trail that cut through raspberry bushes screening the out-house. The table, with a vertical hardwood clamp in the centre and a low seat at one end, was designed specifically for drawknife work. Beside the work table was a stump two feet high with a flat surface. Leaning against the stump was a heavy maple mall, almost as big around as the stump.

The mall and the stump were used to pound wood into thin splints, which were then soaked and shaved smooth and sliced to a specific width. They were soaked again and woven into baskets. Lying around the work table were several different basket molds. Soaking in a galvanized tub filled with water, were splintered spruce roots, ash splints and sweetgrass. On a low rack, made out of woven alder, was seewead drying, to be used for insulation inside the house.

He was glad to be working on something different. He needed a break from clearing the woods – not a complete break though – but another project instead; something to keep him from falling asleep. The thought of doing a new project excited him and banished weariness. The unseen web of nightmares and evil that oppressed and hovered around him seemed to draw back.

Megwadesk set his tool box on the grass and began working. With the axe he split the curved maple into two pieces, which he then roughly shaped into rockers. Then he sat on the work table and did the finer work on the drawknife. Mosquitoes were always more troublesome after a shower. Megwadesk kept swatting them. Once his sweat began pouring from pulling on the drawknife, he no longer felt their bites.

Megwadesk thought of how he hoped to build a work shed one day. By then they would have a proper stove with an oven and he could move the fifty-gallon make-shift stove into the shed. He could work throughout the long, cold, snowy season in perfect comfort and without danger of accidentally hitting the young one.

The young one, yes, the young one, thought Megwadesk. And he felt despair. He remembered seeing Little Molly and wondered again if she had already experienced the injury of raving people throwing rocks at her. Could he protect his child from such madness? There were people out there who would stop at nothing to crush another person's spirit. There were people out there who were determined to take everything away from the Micmacs and leave them begging. There were people out there who came to the reserves and took little ones and sent them off to residential schools. It seemed to him an even harder life awaited his child if he did not make up with his father soon. He felt that, somehow, the child's fate would be changed for the better if the child were brought into the world to take his or her place in an united family. This idea lifted his spirits and he felt that not everything was out of his control. There was something he could do to make life better for the coming child. He remembered Skoltch had automatically assumed it would be a boy. *Well, that's something totally up to the Creator,* he thought. He wished only for a healthy child.

"Yes," he said, "either I make peace with my father or the child will have it even harder in life."

Megwadesk thought happily about how he would tell the little one stories of magic – stories about bugladymúchk, the little people; stories about mígymwesu, the flute-playing wizard of the woods; stories about the supernatural twins, Glúskeb and Malsum, good and evil respectively; stories about Winpi, the northern wizard; stories about Bull Frog's greed; stories about jenúg and gugwesk, the swamp giants and the man-eating giants; stories about jibichgám, the two-horned giant serpent; stories about glu, the flying monster; stories about Dunél, the ancient one, the one who came even before Glúskeb; stories about Babkutbalud, the keeper of souls; stories about Wabus and Gwimu, the messengers . . . and then Megwadesk laughed. He would even tell the little one the story about Glúskeb, Jesus and the Christian messengers that Skoltch had told. Suddenly the troubling question about the origin of spirit stories returned and he stopped laughing.

Wasn't he ultimately responsible for putting ideas into his child's head? How much, he asked himself, *of the past is good to keep, anyway? If them witch tales can stop me from doing things, stop me from doing what I know to be better,* he reasoned, *then, if I told my child the same old silly stories, won't he, too, grow up to be bothered by 'em? But isn't it good to make the most of innocence while it lasts, eh, to make childhood special with wonder 'n' magic? Or is it better to get a child ready for the hurts in the real world by telling the little one how things really are, eh? But then – if he don't have magic – what will a child have to make his world feel good, even when it's going bad? Ah, but I'm making my responsibility as a father too hard! Moquá! I shouldn't worry so much.*

He slowly and painfully uncurled his fingers to release the drawknife. The hands were numb from tightly gripping the drawknife handles for so long. His bruised left forearm made the resurging blood course more painfully than usual through the fingers of his left hand. He reached over to his tool box and took out the pencil and the crooked knife. He drew a floral pattern on the outside face of each rocker and then drew the sun on one and the moon on the other. With his crooked knife, he carved out the pattern. After that, he took a piece of broken glass, holding it in his fingers with the help of a small piece of leather, and gave the rockers a smoother finish by shaving them with the glass edge. Strands of wood almost as fine as hair curled from the glass as he scraped it over the wood. Megwadesk completed the job with sandpaper. Then with the handsaw he trimmed the ends of the rockers square and flush with each other.

Now that he had his rockers, he was happy because he could begin the frame of the cradle itself. However, since he could not attach the frame right away, he put the rockers into the galvanized tub filled with water to soak for a few days. He thought of how when hardwood was wet, it was easier to drive nails into it but then as it dried, the wood shrank and gripped the nails even harder. He smiled, thinking that that was the secret. Otherwise one ended by pounding nails into stubborn wood more likely to split than to accommodate a small puncture.

Dad's like stubborn wood, he thought. *He'd first split up the family, eh, than give a little space to something different than his beliefs like me and Mimi shacking up.*

In an hour Megwadesk finished the frame from pieces of a pine plank. He was about to carve some decorations on it when the brisk and merry strain of the Spring Chicken Reel made him put his tools aside. Apparently Mimi had just returned and did not realize Megwadesk was working in the back yard. Megwadesk listened. The sound coming from the fiddle was thrilling.

He listened to one of Mimi's favourite embellishments, which was to attack two low notes at once, to create dissonance, and then slide up dead on pitch to a sweetly sustained high note. He was familiar with how easily she put the listeners momentarily on edge only to disarm them of their tension with an exact measure of honey. He knew that it was this wonderful mixture of tension and flow that made one jump and dance. He heard another of Mimi's favourite tricks, in which she made the bow bounce carelessly over the strings at the most risky part of the song, making the fiddle stutter, only to return effortlessly to the melody. He enjoyed her spontaneous touches. They were so fluidly and cleverly braided into the main strands of the song that the average listener, while feeling the playing style to be superior, found it difficult to explain what made it so special.

Megwadesk, sitting on the work table, tapped his right foot to the beat and pretended to be playing spoons. Then Mimi slipped into a key one step higher and Megwadesk jumped out of his seat and danced for a couple measures. It was impossible for him to be just a spectator any longer! He ran to the front of the house.

He entered the house, swaying to the rhythm. When Mimi noticed him, he circled his hand through the air, a signal for her to continue playing. He danced, keeping his back very straight, while his legs tangled and untangled. He yelled, "Hoo-wee!" before he hopped over to the corner and picked up his guitar. Mimi smiled and continued playing.

Megwadesk sat by the little table before the window. He sent a cursory glance to a basket of food beside the pail of flour on the table. He wondered where this basket of food had come from. *Mimi must've had more luck than I, getting food*, he thought. Once Megwadesk was strumming the rhythm, Mimi soared into the high harmony line. Megwadesk chuckled at this delightful shift. He tried to throw in the occasional melody line to his chording to complement Mimi's harmony but his hands felt too stiff from using the drawknife.

He watched Mimi. It seemed to him that she looked like a girl of fifteen when she smiled and played the fiddle. Her upper body swayed slightly and her head kept time, her hair shaking like the northern lights. Mimi rounded out the reel by hand-plucking the last notes. She accented the last beat with a loud stomp, which Megwadesk accompanied with his own closing stomp.

After she had set the fiddle on her sewing table, Mimi stood up and asked, a little breathless from laughing, "You know what happened today?"

Megwadesk thought she was the perfect picture of happiness and health. He imagined kissing her and then burying his face between her warm heaving breasts, which filled out the front of her white blouse, and then taking her by the hand and walking outside to kiss again under the bright sun. It was a day to be active, he thought, to maybe take a trip on the boat – a day to look closely into her smiling eyes and see the reflected gleaming wavelets of the river playing there.

"Tell me," he answered.

"It's good news and bad news," Mimi said.

"Well, it's either good news or it's bad news, eh," corrected Megwadesk. "It can't be both."

"Amudj gadu! It can be both good news and bad news at once," Mimi answered, laughing at him. "Not all things are black and white, you know," she reminded him.

"They should be. Then you'd know exactly where you stand."

"Yes, well, this is how it is," Mimi proceeded, grabbing a brush and began stroking her hair. "You know the big cross at the graveyard? It got struck down by lightning. That's the bad news, okay. Now the good news is your father's been hired to build a new cross. When I was saw your parents this morning – "

"What?" Megwadesk exclaimed.

"You think just because you're too proud and too stubborn to talk to your parents, I won't talk to them, either" Mimi asked. "Nisgam! One mule in the house is enough already! I've been visiting your family every morning for a week now! Ána dóq, where was I? Okay, like I was saying, while I was talking to your parents, Peter Algumid came in to see your father. He told him the cross was down and there was no time to waste. A new one has to be erected before St. Anne's Day celebrations. So your father volunteered to do it, as long as the lumber was provided. Peter Algumid insisted your father would get paid."

"I don't see what the good news is," Megwadesk said. "More work for dad, is all." But his voice droned for his thoughts were preoccupied with the surprising revelation that Mimi had been seeing his parents.

"The thing is, dad can't do it by himself. He's got too many things to look after. So dad wants you to build the new cross under his guidance," she said.

Mimi's smile broadened as she studied Megwadesk's face. Her white teeth gleamed like the guitar's ivory inlay. Megwadesk raised the guitar from his lap and slowly set it on the table beside him. He had to push the basket of food and the pail of flour aside.

"Now you get it?" Mimi asked. She put the brush aside and began braiding her hair.

Megwadesk thought he understood all right. His father, in his indirect way, was extending an apology. That was good news certainly, he thought. He realized, though, that what amazed him most was the irony of Mimi bridging the gap between him and his father, when it was his fidelity to Mimi that, in the first place, had made it impossible for him to have anything more to do with his father. Indeed, he thought, Mimi was exactly what he needed to complete himself. He felt Mimi's joy and pride at mending the rupture in his family and it was contagious.

"I'll do it!" Megwadesk said.

"Of course you will," Mimi said. "It's not only some extra money but it means good luck, too. Like they say, 'The one who builds a shrine will be blessed.'"

"Did dad say when he'll start?"

"The day after tomorrow. He said they probably won't bring him the lumber until tomorrow afternoon. Peter Algumid's like that, dad said, always rushing around like a big shot – 'This got to be done right away!' – but then he always leaves his end of the deal for last!"

Mimi laughed again. She said, "Don't look so surprised, dear! It wasn't so hard for me to talk to your father. You and your father are alike in many ways. You both talk as though everything has to be just so, but, of course, nothing's ever like that. Still you have to believe it's just so. Then when you say something wrong, you can't take it back, and somebody else has to take the first step to make things right again. Men and their pride! It's so stupid! Now you can't tell me you haven't been missing your father! Nisgam! You walk around like a lost child. Bana, you don't even notice things around you any more! I couldn't take another day of it!"

"How did my father act, eh?"

"You mean the first time I went to see them? Oh, he was happy! He cupped my hand with both hands and asked me how you were doing. And when it was clear to both your parents we were having some hard luck, your father wanted to help us right away. But I told them you were still sensitive about getting any help from them."

Megwadesk hesitated, and then he blurted, "Did you tell them?"

"Yes. This morning. After I told you. Your mum was surprised. I got the feeling dad expected the news, though. He just laughed and right away he stood up and started stuffing a basket with food. 'You're eating for two now,' he said. That's the basket, right there beside you! He said I couldn't say no. Don't fuss! He said if you objected, then don't call it a gift, but an advance from the work you'll be doing for him. Then your mum gave me all the old advice. 'Always try to stay cheerful,' she said, 'and don't stand around on thresholds or in doorways! My God, that's the most dangerous place for a pregnant woman, especially if it's the house of a buowin!'"

"How 'bout your parents, eh? Have you told 'em already?"

"My mum's known a long time now, you crazy! Who do you think's been giving me all the advice? I'm sure she's written to dad about it already."

"They had a postal strike in June," Megwadesk said.

"Only for ten days."

Mimi paused. Her expression became grave. Megwadesk read her eyes and asked, "They weren't happy about our plans, eh?"

"My mum told me, 'I wish I had your courage when I was your age. I let that priest bully us around. Thank God, you never buckled under him! I hate to think how sad you could've made our lives.' Mum doesn't blame me at all but your parents tried to talk me out of it. They didn't press me, though. Your father clenched his hands when I told them about it. So I said right away, 'Listen, I'm not going to let my child go through the same thing I did! Nisgam, the priest wouldn't marry my parents when my mum was going to have me, so why should he marry me and your son? It's the same situation. Only difference is we're not going to be held hostage by religion. If we have to get married through another church, that's fine!' And they said they understood, but they also added that Father Colérique is a changed man.

"So I said, 'Nothing can change what he's done! He damned innocent children and ruined them! I'm sure he's upset I didn't turn out like the other girls!' Then they tried

78

to, well, they tried to bribe me like. Your mum said, 'We'll help with all the expenses, if you'll let the priest marry you.' I told her we'd manage all alone if we had to.

"Boys, she got me mad when she said, 'You're just doing this out of spite. If you cared for your little one, you would know that other children will taunt her for belonging to a different religion. She won't fit in. When all the other kids are practising for Holy Confirmation, she'll be left out.'"

"She's right, dear," Megwadesk said.

"I told her, 'I survived being called a bastard all these years and it made me tough. My kid will grow up tough, too!' She said, 'Well, if you want her to grow up tough and to be called names all the time, then just don't get married.' I said, 'Listen, we're getting married and that priest isn't going to have a thing to do with it. That's it!' So your mum said that Father Colérique isn't the only Catholic priest in the world. Anyway, she's going to visit us tomorrow to find out how our meeting with the preacher went."

"That's not how it ended, eh."

Mimi tied her braids.

"No. We sort of eased away from that issue. Your mum asked if I wanted some coffee and I answered, yes, thanks. Then your father mentioned a warden got beat up this morning."

"Really? Where?"

"You won't believe this! The Nommis boys – Johnny, Nisnus, and Laleve – were about to clean their nets when a warden glided right towards them. Yes! Right in front of the reserve! You know where the Nommis boys set, right."

"Yes, yes," Megwadesk said impatiently, "near the church."

"Yes, just below the church. The warden came right into the reserve on his boat and started untying their nets. He was going to take them."

"Confiscate them?"

"But can you believe it? Nisgam!"

"It's crazy! We can't even fish any more!"

"But how bold! Or how stupid! I don't know which."

"So what happened, eh?"

"Your father said, bana, the boys couldn't believe it, at first. They rowed out on their dories and asked the warden what he was up to. He said he was taking their nets because they didn't have a fishing licence. They told him to stop what he was doing. They even mentioned parts of the *Indian Act*, but the warden didn't know anything about that."

"Of course, he wouldn't. They never do, eh."

"So he tried to push their boats aside and that's when Johnny blew up. Then the other boys got mad, too. They dragged the warden to shore and did a number on him."

"Son of a gun! Those boys are going to get charges laid against them."

"Your father says it's a good thing if it goes to court. We could win an important case. Only problem is he doesn't think the chief and council will back the Nommis boys with a good lawyer."

"No, I don't think so either. They like to keep the money in their pockets, eh. Is that all you heard?"

"No."

"What else did you hear?"

"A little bird in the trees told me something."

"Huh!" Megwadesk stared at Mimi as she walked towards him, her eyes staring steadily into his.

"The little bird told me, 'Your old man's hungry, hungry, hungry! Your old man's hungry for a kiss!'"

Mimi rushed into Megwadesk's arms, and onto his lap. Megwadesk looked at Mimi. He ran his hands up and down her back and sides as they kissed. He kissed her luscious lips and then her left cheek. His trail of kisses traced her jaw and lingered on her throat and slender neck before plunging to her collar bone, further descent deterred by her buttoned blouse.

He settled his head over her breasts and asked, "How many months along are you?"

"Three-and-a-half. God, it scares me sometimes. I dreamt I was very large with child and I took off my blouse to look at my stomach. And then my stomach was just a big blister, filled with nothing but water! Bana, I was so terrified!"

"Oh, it's just a dream."

"But I felt so alone."

Megwadesk calculated that three-and-a-half months ago was just after he had announced to his parents that they planned to shack-up. They had temporarily moved in with

Mimi's mother, while he had built the house.

Mimi ran her fingers through his hair. He asked, raising an eyebrow and smiling roguishly at her, "What else did that clever little bird tell you, hmm? What else am I hungry for, hmm?"

"Nugú!" Mimi exclaimed, getting off his lap, and playfully slapping his shoulder. "I've got a hundred things to do before our guest arrives!"

"Me too," Megwadesk said, grasping her hand. He let himself be pulled to his feet and his hand slid around Mimi's waist. With his other hand he lifted the guitar from the table.

"Aren't you happy?" Mimi asked.

Megwadesk thought, *Well, she's got no idea how little I've slept the past week, eh. Boys, I'm tired!*

"Oh, I'm very happy," he said with a stiff smile. He yawned and rubbed his eyes and then replaced the guitar in the corner.

Chapter Eight

Empty Baskets

Megwadesk did not return his tools inside the house. He collected them in the little tool box and hid them, with the frame of the rocking cradle, on the rack under the rafters in the back of the house. He thought, *I'll surprise Mimi with my work once I've got the rockers on the frame, eh.* He left the rockers soaking in the tub, hidden under the soaking splints.

He walked through wooded trail that descended to the small field by the river. Once he was aboard his scow, he placed the anchor inside the boat and set the box with the old net in it on the deck. He untied the end of the net attached to the rock and dropped this end into the box. Carefully he collected the rest of the net, pulling his boat along in the operation. The net was heavy with filth washed down by rain. Megwadesk took excessive pride in keeping his clothes spotless and dry when he worked on the boat. It was not always possible to stay dry and clean, especially in rough weather, but he did so on this occasion. His sleeves and trousers were rolled up and his bare feet straddled the width of the deck. He kept his back as upright as possible.

He untied the other end of the net from the stake, rowed back to shore, tossed the anchor in the grass, and walked with the box up the bank. He tied one end of the net with a half-hitch knot to a pine bough, seven feet off the ground, and walked thirty yards to a white birch to tie the other end. Then with a long pole, having a branched tip, he hooked the top line of the net about midway its length and pushed it up like a clothesline loaded down with wet clothes. It was up to the sun to do the rest.

He left the old net in the bottom of the box. There was no

fishing thread with which to mend it. He took one end of the old net and pulled it out to examine the holes.

Megwadesk thought, *We all have our webs to tend to, eh.*

He remembered how his father enjoyed telling stories. Looking at his torn net now, the story about Nujísawed his father had told him when he was a boy flashed across Megwadesk's mind.

Nujísawed, his father told him, was a magical being who lived in the Sky-World. His wigwam floated high above the mountains. The poles of his wigwam were rainbows, the walls of his wigwam were woven from sunlight, and the floor of his wigwam was lined with clouds.

Nujísawed had been given his name, which meant One-Who-Weaves, because he wove nets. And the nets that he made reached as high as the Star-World and dropped as deep as earth. With these great nets, Nujísawed caught the rays of the sun and the moon. He made the rays into threads of many colours and he used these shining threads to adorn his clothes.

People on earth could not see the sky nets. Only the Star People could see the great nets Nujísawed made and the Star People decided to descend to earth on the nets. The Star People held their torches between their teeth and crept down the nets. When they reached earth, the Star People raced with each other and played by the river.

The Micmacs, seeing the glowing creatures, exclaimed, "Look! Those are water-spirits! Nothing can be more beautiful than those water-spirits!"

Every night the Star People climbed down the sky nets to visit earth. The Star People climbed up and down the nets so much that they damaged the nets. They broke the mesh with their constant traffic. Nujísawed worked day and night mending his nets.

Sometimes, during the day, Nujísawed would stop his mending and look on earth. He would see the Micmacs hunting. From the sky, Nujísawed saw all the deer yards; he saw the moose haunts; he saw where every game was located. Hunting looked like an easy matter.

Nujísawed thought, "I wouldn't have to work this hard if I lived on earth. I would just hunt. I wouldn't have to keep mending nets. The Star People are a nuisance! If I lived on earth with the Micmacs, I wouldn't have to put up with all the trouble the Star people make for me."

One day Nujísawed grew weary with mending nets. He climbed down to earth and sat on a boulder. After night fall, he watched the Star People climb down his nets. Because he had not mended his nets, many Star People fell through the holes. They dropped from the nets and flew across the night sky to crash into the earth. They were the first shooting stars.

"The earth is a hard place to land when you're going that fast!"Nujísawed shouted and laughed.

Next morning, dressed in his best garments, Nujísawed walked to the village. His jacket and leggings glittered with colourful designs. The people were amazed. Nujísawed told them he was from another nation and that he was looking for a wife. The people welcomed him, of course.

It seemed like everything would go well for Nujísawed but that night, after Nujísawed first entered the village, another stranger – a ginab who moved in darkness – arrived. People immediately sensed power from this new arrival. They sensed his approach even before he reached the village. The people went out to meet this strange ginab. When he was close to the village, the stranger asked to be allowed to set up a wigwam near the river, a short distance from the village. The people could only see his eyes in the darkness but they made him welcome nonetheless, for they were sure he was a ginab – a man possessing mystical powers.

The ginab built his wigwam in darkness. By the time day rolled around, he was already inside. From that day forth, the ginab stayed in his wigwam. Unlike Nujísawed, he did not go out to hunt. At first, people worried that he might starve to death, so hunters left meat by his door but the meat was never taken. Instead, the mysterious stranger told each hunter who brought food to him, "I can tell you where you can find more of that meat."

When a hunter brought a piece of deer meat to the ginab's lodge, the ginab would tell that hunter where there were deer. Before long, hunters were bringing strips of every sort of wild game to the ginab's lodge in order to learn where specific game was to be found. When a family desired some partridge to eat, one of the hunters for that family would take a partridge feather to the ginab's lodge and the power-

ful man would direct the hunter to where there were partridge. And yet – although he never took any of the food
offered to him – the ginab did not perish, as though he had
some magical source of food inside his wigwam. It was rumoured that he had baskets of food that always replenished
their stock when the lids were replaced on them.

Meantime, Nujísawed could not find a wife because he
proved to be a terrible hunter. He knew nothing about track-
ing game. It had all looked so easy from the sky. Walking
through the woods looking for signs on the ground was
another matter.

Nujísawed complained to one of the men that he was
having bad luck in hunting. The man told him, "Go see the
mysterious man, go see the ginab who never comes out of
his wigwam. That man can help you. He helps all the hunters."

So Nujísawed went to the ginab's lodge to ask for help.
The mysterious man, however, would not help him. He
would not even speak to Nujísawed.

Eventually, Nujísawed was forced to make nets and try
his luck at fishing. Perhaps he could catch fish the same
way he used to catch the rays of the sun and the rays of the
moon. To his surprise, his idea worked. Day after day he
hauled in fish of all kinds: striped bass, salmon, trout, mackerel, perch, and still others.

The people were fascinated by his invention. Weirs had
to wait for fish but a net could be taken to where fish were.
Soon people were constantly asking Nujísawed to make nets
for them and soon Nujísawed had no more time to fish. He
became too busy making nets full-time for the people. At
first, he thought if he taught the people how to weave their
nets, he would regain his free time. The people took lessons
from him and learned how to weave nets all right, but they
insisted that his nets were lucky.

"Why do you come to me for nets now?" he complained
to them. "I've already taught you how to make nets. Go
and make your own!"

"Oh, but your nets are special, my friend," would always
be the reply. "Your nets are very lucky!"

There was no getting away from it. The people insisted
that Nujísawed make all the nets. As a result, by constantly

making and mending nets, soon he was hating his work again.

"I'm no better off here than I was in the Sky-World," he grumbled. "I'm always working – always making nets!"

One day the ginab warned the people that if they wanted his power to keep helping them with the hunt, they should have nothing to do with the nets Nujísawed made. The hunters promised the ginab they would not have anything to do with Nujísawed. They thought they could lie to the mysterious man just because he never left his wigwam. When they asked Nujísawed to make them nets, the ginab knew.

He told the hunters, one by one as they came to his lodge, "You lacked nothing when you depended on me, so why have you gone to Nujísawed for help? I cannot help you any longer."

Soon after that, a terrible thing happened throughout the land. Everything changed. The winter was dry and cold; spring was short; summer was hot; crops would not flower; grass turned brown; rivers dried up; and fishing was not good. Even the animals disappeared. The hunters searched everywhere and still returned empty-handed. There was famine. The people were finally left with no choice but to tear their leather clothing and boil it to make a poor broth. Even Nujísawed had to boil his beautiful jacket and leggings. There was nothing else left to eat. The people drank water until their arms and legs became skinny and their stomachs grew bloated.

"I wish I were back in the Sky-World," thought Nujísawed, but he could not go back. He had neglected the sky nets for so long that they rotted away.

One night the people went to the ginab's lodge. They wanted help from him. The ginab told them they could open the door but that they could not come into the lodge.

The people opened the door and asked him, "Why are these terrible things happening to us?"

Only the ginab's eyes could be seen blazing from within. His face remained indistinct for the sputtering fire before him was nothing more than ashes. The ginab answered, "All things are connected just like the strings that make up a net are all connected. A man should never leave gaps in his net. He should always mend his net if he wants to stay in good relation to the world. If there are gaps in the net then those gaps will affect the whole net. Fish will go through those gaps. That is the same between the Earth-World and the Sky-World. When something is missing in one place, it will affect the other place. I tell you now that something is missing in the Sky-World. That is all I will say."

The ginab then gave Nujísawed a penetrating look.

Nujísawed backed away from the ginab's wigwam. All along, the ginab had known who Nujísawed was! Nujísawed walked to the woods and then fled from the village. He went north. He could walk only a short distance each day for he was too weak. For days he walked through the dry forest. One night, Nujísawed lay down on a bed of pine needles and wept. He was hungry and tired. He looked at his skinny arms and his skinny legs. He looked at his bloated stomach.

He thought, "I used to be the best-looking man in all the worlds. Now look at me!"

He lay on the ground until darkness covered the world. He decided to die. The forest was quiet. No owl called; no deer whistled; no partridge drummed. It was as dark and as quiet as a cave. Suddenly Nujísawed heard something. Snap!Ssshhheee – BUMP! Snap! Ssshhheee – BUMP!

It sounded like somebody was walking with one good foot and one bad foot. He was stepping on twigs as he went and dragging his foot behind. Nujísawed looked in the direction of the sound of the footsteps. Through the trees he could see a light going on and off. At first, Nujísawed thought that the light was going on and off because the man kept disappearing behind trees and reappearing again. Nujísawed followed the man with the light.

The man had one stiff leg and twisted arms. His face was scarred, his nose was broken, and one eye was lower than the other. He was hunchbacked, too. At the top of his hump sat a stone dish that cradled a bed of coals. The coals kept glowing and dimming and glowing again. Nujísawed followed the hunchback until the hunchback went inside a wigwam that stood beside a lake.

Nujísawed went to the wigwam and shouted the old Micmac greeting, "Kwéi!"

The hunchback answered, "Come in! Have the seat of

honour."

When Nujísawed walked in, the hunchback exclaimed, "Who walks in looking so sick?"

Nujísawed answered, "To look at me now, you would never guess that I was once the most handsome man in all the worlds. Don't tell anyone, but I used to be the Net-Weaver of the Sky-World. My name is Nujísawed."

The hunchback's eyes sparkled. A grin spread across his face. He said, "And you can call me Hunchback. What can Hunchback do for you?"

Nujísawed said he was hungry. Hunchback served Nujísawed a meal of potatoes, venison, corn-bread and strawberries. Nujísawed ate until he was full and then he fell asleep. The next morning, Hunchback gave Nujísawed three basketfuls of food.

Hunchback said, "One is full of wild fruits. The other has vegetables. The last has meat and fish. These baskets will never run out of food. You can take all you want from them and the baskets will refill. But listen carefully! These magical baskets will not work if you open them before you get back to your village. The food is for everyone. Do not open them until you get back to the village!"

Hunchback gave Nujísawed a leather back-pack to carry all three baskets. Nujísawed started back to the village. He was happy, thinking, "From now on, I'll never have to make another net and the people will never have to hunt or fish again! These three baskets will sustain me and my people!"

All day he walked southward. Sometimes he heard a twig snap behind him. Nujísawed felt strong because he had eaten the previous night. He could walk in one day what before had taken him many days to walk. Finally, he got tired. It was night. He was hungry. The aroma of the juicy meat, berries, and boiled corn from the baskets drove him crazy. He opened the baskets and devoured everything. Sometimes he thought he heard someone chuckling in the woods. He closed the baskets and fell asleep.

Next morning, he woke up and opened the baskets. They were full of food.

"Good! I did not destroy the magic," he said.

He continued walking all that day. In the evening he made it to the village. Before he walked into the village, he hung the baskets on some branches. He wanted to surprise the people. He ran into the village. The people were surprised to see him move with so much energy.

"I have great news!" he shouted. "I have found food! Come with me, for I have found food!"

As Nujísawed told them of the delicious food he had eaten, the people became enraptured. They could see in their minds thick slices of deer meat, bowls filled with sweet corn and heapings of juicy strawberries. Nujísawed took them to where the baskets hung on the branches.

"Open those baskets," he said. "There's all kinds of food in them!"

The people opened the first basket. It was empty. The people opened the second basket. It was empty. The people rushed over to the third basket and opened it. There was nothing in that one, either.

The people were so enraged that they attacked Nujísawed. They beat him with sticks and then they took stone axes and split each of his arms and each of his legs. By then they were all exhausted and so they left him to bleed to death. It was night again and Nujísawed was barely alive.

Hunchback had watched from the woods. Hunchback came out and laughed at Nujísawed.

He said, "I can leave you here to die or I can help you. Do you want to live?"

"Yes," replied Nujísawed.

"Well, then, I will help you!"

Hunchback's stone dish of coal glowed and its light grew stronger until it was as bright as the sun. He seized Nujísawed's head in his hands and pressed and shrank Nujísawed until he was no bigger than a finger nail.

The light from the stone dish subsided again, and Hunchback said, "Your new name is Awógejid, Spider. Your split arms and split legs are now eight legs. You will always have a bloated stomach. And you can never again make nets from the ground up. You will always have to swing down to earth to make them. That way you can never return to the Sky-World."

Hunchback set Spider on the ground.

He continued, "I used to live in the Star-World until I fell through a net you hadn't repaired. I broke every bone in the fall and even my torch doesn't work right any more. Stay here. I'll soon be back to tell you more. But first I must go see the people."

Hunchback walked to the village. The dejected people did not even have any fires going. They lay around the wigwams, utterly exhausted and groaning, their faces like skulls under the moon light.

Hunchback told them, "I have come from the lodge of the ginab. He has left this area. Before he left, he told me to tell you that the true baskets of food are to be found in his lodge. Go there and you will find food and things that will help you."

The people went to the lodge that stood alone by the river. At first they feared to enter. They called out, "Kwéi," but nobody answered. Finally they stepped in. There was no one in the lodge. Inside were baskets of food and there were other baskets filled with nets. The people rejoiced.

Meantime Hunchback walked back to where Spider sat. Again the bed of coals on Hunchback's stone dish became radiant and then the light began to dim. This time as the light dimmed, the Hunchback shrank and shrank until he was no bigger than Spider. Hunchback looked at the man who used to be the Net-Weaver and said, "You asked me for my name once. My name is Wasoqejid. I am firefly." And firefly flew away into the forest, his light going on and off.

Megwadesk's father had concluded this story, as he did with all his stories, by saying, "Gesbiaduksid," which was the traditional way to close a story. It literally meant, "He has come to the end of his tale." Megwadesk remembered how he used to wonder, as a boy, why storytellers did not close with "Gesbiaduksi," which meant, "I have come to the end of my tale," but he had realized much later that storytellers could not give themselves credit because they imagined the story to come from something else out there.

Then he pondered on the story. *Are we all like Nujísawed?* he wondered. *Are we all tied to our tasks, eh? It's like he fell from heaven to hell on 'count he didn't like his task! He wanted to be free, eh, but nobody's free 'tall. If a man can't do what he likes, well, then, least you'd think he'd be free to think as he likes. But that ain't so neither! Just think 'bout a man trying to hold one thing in his mind for an hour, eh. Why, just a small thing like dirt getting blown in his eyes'll make 'im forget 'bout what he was trying to hold in mind 'n' get 'im to start swearing 'n' to start figuring out how he's gonna clean his eye out. Think, they tell you, before you act, eh, but before you realize it, your thoughts've already run off to the direction they're most used to taking off to. So a suspicious man gets suspicious when something happens 'n' an angry man gets angry. But still both of 'em are thinking, 'cept neither's got any control over where their thoughts are going. But don't that excuse everything, eh? If there ain't no free will, then everything's fated 'n' every crime can be excused 'cause it was fated. So the whites can say they stole our land but that was just meant to be so there's nothing 'tall wrong with it! But that's crazy! We're left with empty baskets. Yet everything's really just a reaction to everything else, and how much of this do we got control over?*

Megwadesk waded into the river and washed his rough hands and then he sat on a flat stump and smoked his pipe. A pair of butterflies tumbled silently over the clumps of raspberry bushes and the scattered stunted fir. They erratically lifted again and then settled on the flowers of the wild rosebush leaning over the bank. Megwadesk walked to the rosebush. He saw a spider swinging down a stem. He plucked the petals from a rose and tossed them on the water.

"Children are petals on the river," he thought. From a nearby fir, where it had perched so quietly in the shade of the branches that Megwadesk had not noticed it before, a sparrow darted out and snatched the spider.

Megwadesk was hungry. He had not had much to eat that morning and much of his energy had gone into carving the rockers and making the cradle. He walked to the shore. As he strode through the tall grass, he disturbed hundreds of grasshoppers. When he reached the shore, he saw a great blue heron gliding over the water as majestical, he thought, as an infant's memory of huge, slow-moving worlds.

Megwadesk got a bucket and a shovel from his boat and dug some clams. He made a fire, boiled the clams, and ate as many as he needed to get the edge out of his hunger. Then he cut some switches of very straight maple shoots. He walked back to his dried net and whipped it. The dried moss and seaweed flew off as he lashed the net.

He thought of what his father had told him. "A net likes to be kept clean," his father had said. "It works harder for you when you treat it well and keep it clean. But never use crooked switches. A net doesn't like to be threatened with sharp edges that can tear or tangle it. Only use very straight switches, and then you can lash your net hard and it won't care. It'll be happy because you're washing its hands. Ash is best, but maple's good, too."

Just before he reset his net, he took a hammer and went around his boat, hitting any nail that stuck out so his net would not get snagged and rip. When he had set his net, Megwadesk felt proud. His net was clean. The string of white floats leaped lightly over the wavelets one after another. He looked at the line of moss indicating his neighbour's net. Skoltch had not yet cleaned his net. Megwadesk wished he could have blamed this neglect on Skoltch's laziness but he knew better. Skoltch was probably in Trenton, selling his catch.

Chapter Nine

Superstition and Resolution

The door was open to cool the house after Mimi's cooking and Megwadesk, seated by the table, looked out the window. Several minutes ago he had seen a familiar boat sailing into the cove. Soon a lanky, black shape strode briskly, almost scuttled, over the front clearing. Megwadesk got the same impression each time he studied the preacher's stiff upper-body, the impression that Mr. Severman slept in his clothes suspended against the wall, underarms hooked over large wooden pegs. The preacher's broad and bony shoulders curled up towards the wide brim of his hat and his pointy elbows jutted out to the sides. *Then again*, Megwadesk imagined, *maybe his wife hangs him on the clothesline every so often, eh, pinned by the shoulders 'n' again by the elbows.* Mr. Severman's thin arms were so long that his elbows almost reached his knees. He walked with his knees and his toes pointed out. He was a blur of angles, joints, and limbs as he hurried towards the house. Mr. Severman reminded Megwadesk of the spider, big-daddy-long-legs. He knew that the preacher was in his early fifties although he had the energy and expression of a thirty year old.

Since Megwadesk associated black with Father Colérique, and since Father Colérique always wore a severe expression, it was always difficult for Megwadesk to imagine a kindly face hidden in the shadows of the preacher's big black hat. Yet Mr. Severman was a gentle-looking man. Megwadesk wondered if his large cow-like eyes were the result of his diet. He knew that Mr. Severman was a vegetarian.

"He's here," Megwadesk told Mimi.

Mimi, coming out of their bedroom, asked, "How do I look?"

Mimi had on her hand-made emerald silk dress. Traditional geometric designs cut from colourful ribbons were sown into the dress. Her hair, which was unbraided and wavy, was tied in the back by ribbons as well. She wore earrings of silver and purple amethyst. A loosely knotted blue scarf with fringes on its edges went around her neck. Her loose blouse was saffron and the airy sleeves flowed over the cuffs. Three decorative silver plates attached to a silver necklace hung just below her scarf. These trade items were older than anything Megwadesk had, going as far back as the early days of the Seven Years War. Mimi smelled of the sweetgrass she hung in her clothes closet.

"Gisúlk! You look like I oughta take you down the aisle this minute, eh!" Megwadesk replied. Although they already lived together, the idea of marriage excited Megwadesk. A ceremony put a magical touch to whatever it concerned.

"You look kind of handsome, too,"Mimi replied, smiling.

Megwadesk had greased and neatly parted his hair. He wore a tie, a white cotton shirt, dark blue dress pants with blue suspenders, and black shoes. He cupped in his palms the large silver medallion and the smaller bronze medallion hanging from his neck. He made sure they were neatly hanging from their ribbons.

There was a knock.

Mimi waved Mr. Severman in, saying, "Ybchilásij, jínyma," which meant, "Let the man enter and have the seat of honour." Mr. Severman already understood quite a few Micmac expressions.

When he walked in and saw how the young couple were dressed, they knew he could see that his visit would not turn out to be just another routine call. He seemed self-conscious, perhaps because his dusty garb did not measure up to the occasion – whatever it would be. He hastily removed his hat and said, automatically, "Ma'am." He was usually on familiar terms with both Mimi and Megwadesk but their surprising transformation now compelled a formal address.

His brown hair was sweaty and he combed it back with his hands. The way his short hair streamed together into so many feathers reminded Megwadesk of wet muskrat fur.

"Let me take your jacket," Mimi said, taking his hat and then helping him out of his jacket, which she then hung on the same spike Megwadesk's jacket hung.

"Imagine a servant waited on by a queen! That's how you make me feel just now, Mimi. Terribly awkward," Mr. Severman said and Mimi laughed. "Yes! You two certainly look grand this evening!" He tugged at the cuffs of his black shirt to work the wrinkles out of the sleeves.

Megwadesk approached him and shook his hand, saying, "You look grand, too, Mr. Severman."

"Oh, you certainly don't lack in charity, Megwadesk! But I have a feeling there's a devil in you who revels in irony, huh! I know full well how plain I look beside you two. Never more so than now! So, tell me, what is the occasion? Mimi, you are always a beauty to behold – however humbly you may be arrayed, nothing can diminish the radiance of your smile so delightfully emphasized in those sweet brackets that are your dimples – but, Megwadesk, why, I've never seen you so regal! And those medals – what do they signify? I must say, I am altogether mystified!"

Megwadesk walked Mr. Severman to the table and pulled a chair for him. He felt proud, hearing the medallions clinking on his chest.

Megwadesk took a seat. He raised the bronze medallion with his left hand and said, "Sir, this medal was given to my great-great-grandfather, eh, Peter Ligasudi, by the King of England at that time, King George. Our delegation, the Micmacs, went to England. This was when the Bostoners fought each other, eh."

"The American Revolution, yes," said the preacher.

Then Megwadesk raised the silver medallion even higher with his right hand and added, "An' this one was given to him by George Washington. Both sides, eh, wanted us either on their side or totally out of the war!"

Megwadesk solemnly nodded, sure he had explained everything. Even presidents and kings acknowledged the importance of his lineage. When Mr. Severman corrugated his forehead with eyebrows raised in surprise,

Megwadesk beamed.

Mimi served dinner and the three of them ate. Megwadesk did not eat much so that Mr. Severman would be feasted. During their meal, Mimi explained to Mr. Severman that, as he already knew, she was interested in converting to his church. She wanted to know if he could marry a couple when one of them was not a member of his church. He said he could do so. Mimi then said she was prepared to convert within a month and she and Megwadesk wished to be married within two months. Mr. Severman was delighted.

"This is, indeed, a special occasion!" he intoned.

Mimi and Megwadesk agreed that Mr. Severman had a way of making English sound almost as musical as Micmac. Mr. Severman raised his cup of tea and the three of them toasted. Mr. Severman wanted to know more about the medallions and this led to a discussion on Micmac history, which in turn veered off to a discussion about Micmac legends. Mimi finished her meal and left the table, letting the men talk while she went to work on the quilt for the baby. Still, she kept an ear on their discussion.

"But I wonder 'bout them old stories sometimes, eh," Megwadesk said. "Some of them deal with history, true 'nough, but then they include all kinds of magic. Take Melkabilasid, for example. They say he was the war chief who, 'long with Algimu, drove the Gwedejk back."

"What does his name mean? Milky – what was it?"

"Meeel-kaaa-biiil-aaa-siiid. It means Tied-In-A-Strong-Knot. He lived way, way before the time of Columbus! The Micmacs 'n' the Gwedejk used to live like brothers, eh, but then bitter feelings started over a lacrosse game, because some guys got killed. Lacrosse used to be rough, eh! Well, there were three wars."

Megwadesk outlined the story about the wars. He knew from previous visits that if Mr. Severman was interested in the story he would come back another time and ask for more details. He also understood that Mr. Severman rarely asked for details on the first telling of any story because it was easier for him to remember an outline first and then to add details to it later.

"Only in the third war, eh," Megwadesk concluded, "did

a leader come 'long who could lead the Micmacs to victory. That was Algimu 'n' he made Melkabilasid his war chief. Together, the two brothers, the ginab 'n' the great war chief, drove the Iroquois back, eh, year after year. Algimu lived to be an old man an', one winter, he asked his people, when he was 'bout to die, eh, to set his body up in the trees, promising he'd come 'live again the next spring. So the people, after he died, set his body on the trees 'n' left 'im there. Come spring, sure 'nough, eh, they see'm walking 'round, but one of his cheeks is chewed up pretty bad – s'pose by a weasel while his body was dead, eh. The second time Algimu died, they buried him. Algimu promised this time he'd live with the Micmacs forever if they dug him out of his grave the next day. He told the people, eh, he told 'em the sign that his spirit be returned to his body'd be a bolt of thunder tearing the clear sky. That'd be the sign, eh, a thunderbolt without clouds, the sign for the people to dig his body outa the grave. But, once Algimu was buried, the chiefs, they got together 'n' said, 'Hey, let's not dig 'im out tomorrow. He'll be too powerful. We'll have no control over 'im 'tall. Maybe he'll turn 'gainst us.' The chiefs were 'fraid to lose all the power, you see, but their excuse to the people was, 'We won't never learn to stand on our own two feet 'tall if we keep relying on Algimu.' An' so they piled even more stones over his body, eh, making a mound. So next day there was a thunderbolt in a clear sky but they didn't dig 'im out. An' that was that. They say Algimu's still breathing in his grave in Amherst Point, waiting to come out to make war again."

"Fascinating!" Mr. Severman said.

"My point is, that story has history, eh. But it's like a tall tale, too."

"Sure. Superstition has to be mingled with fact. All primitive societies rely heavily on superstitious dread to keep their people in line," Mr. Severman said.

"That's what it is!" Megwadesk cried excitedly. "That's the word, eh – superstition! Did you hear that, Mimi? Superstition! There's still lots of it 'round, even today!"

"Oh, certainly, certainly," Mr. Severman nodded, his fingers laced together over his stuffed stomach.

Megwadesk found in Mr. Severman the audience he had long wanted. He gave vent to his idea that many spirit stories were superstitions. He told Mr. Severman about the man in white and how the strange calm of that night had made him think he was hearing ghosts. Then he said trees creaking in the breeze probably inspired the story about mígymwesu, the flute-playing wizard of the woods. And he mentioned Wejúsyn, the great bird who created storms with his wings. One of the Micmacs walking through the woods one day had probably felt the breeze from the wings of a low flying raven and that had explained to him the origin of wind. Mr. Severman, who did not know a great deal about Micmac mythology, mentioned examples from other native groups. He discussed the Windigo at great length.

Megwadesk did not know anything about the Windigo but he kept nodding, thinking, "Yes, it's all just superstitions – only nonsense, eh – an' I won't have nothing to fear tonight."

Megwadesk pictured himself rowing through darkness to Skoltch's net. He kept nodding as Mr. Severman expounded his ideas but Megwadesk had his gaze on an internal vision.

The sun was low when Mr. Severman announced he had to leave. As was his tradition, he pulled several sheets of paper from his shirt pocket, unfolded them, and said, "But before I go, I must, in turn, leave you with a story."

Mimi stood up and poured herself another cup of tea and sat again to listen to Mr. Severman's story.

Mr. Severman winked at Megwadesk. He said, "Here's my latest fabrication – a real dandy. Imagine, if you will, a spider talking. Yes! A spider! A wonderful image, isn't it? I can see you're struck dumb, Megwadesk."

Megwadesk said, "Well, it's 'cause I know a good story 'bout a spider, too."

"Oh, I know! You told it to me once. In fact, that story with something else we once discussed, when you were teaching me the finer points of sailing, inspired the piece I'm about to read. Do you remember the time you told me about how beauty and innocence sometimes affected you? You laughed when I called you an artist. Your reply was that you never painted – remember?"

"Yes! Oh, yes! He called me an artist, Mimi. Can you believe that, eh? An' I said you're the artist in the house, not me!"

"And I explained to him, Mimi, that I had meant he had the *soul* and the *sensitivity* of an artist. Anyway, our discussion on beauty made a strong impression on me. I knew that we had touched on a fundamental issue in art and, when I returned to my house, I started writing and continued writing until I came up with this story."

Mr. Severman's brows pressed heavily over his eyes and he pursed his mouth; then he added, "Oh, how I wish I could read this stuff in church sometimes! I get so weary of those moralizing sermons! Really, I just don't know any more if I believe in my vocation. Sometimes – frequently, in fact – I catch myself wishing that when I was young, I had pursued another – oh, never mind! I am too old to dream of other things, and grieve my lost courage! I am what I am now. That's how some lives turn out. But, I'm rambling. Well, so this story is in the voice of a spider."

Mr. Severman swallowed some water, set his cup back on the table, and cleared his throat. Mimi and Megwadesk waited. Mr. Severman's stories were always entertaining. They were usually about a comical character named Pastor Duncan. This time, though, the couple sensed something much more than just a story in the air. Mr. Severman seemed troubled. The preacher read.

"'Life, when it is just survival, can be ugly,'" he began reading, but he stopped and said, "Oh, I'm sorry. I forgot to mention the title. I call it *Webs*. So let me begin again."

"'Life, when it is just survival, can be ugly. Life must have beauty. I am immersed in beauty. I am forever spinning beauty from my flesh. Nowadays my purpose in spinning webs is not merely to catch flies any more. Now my concern for food is almost incidental to the act of weaving a web. I love the feeling of being lost in imagination for days, recalculating the design of a work in progress with every shift in the breeze. Marvellous structures are woven and unwoven in my mind as I release filament and descend. Each web is a surprise. I never know what shape it will finally acquire.

"'Once the web is finished, I stand in one of its corners and contemplate it, marvelling at the results of a genius that has spontaneously responded to every change in the weather. I am not boasting. All spiders are possessed when engaged in the act of weaving. We enter a trance and dance with creation. The genius is never ours. We disappear from the world of appetite and enter pure abstraction. We are only instruments. The web is the product of something much greater than ourselves.

"'I get upset when a fly lands on the web soon after its completion. I need time to concentrate on the undisturbed web. We believe that in contemplating webs the fullness of appreciation eventually blooms into realizations. Ideally, each web should yield a truth. But survival being what it is – so full of chaos and so contrary to design – it is rare that any series of webs will deliver their true potential. More likely than not a fly will crash into the web soon after its completion. How disturbing such moments are! How profoundly disturbing! On the one hand, there is this thrill in catching the next meal but, on the other hand, there is this extreme sense of violation as a part of oneself is rent to threads by the thrashings of a fly.

"'These moments are disturbing because they overwhelm us with those eternal questions. What is life, if it is not to be in the knowing of wonders? Why, then, does life interrupt itself? Why must the process of knowing be rudely dashed by matters of appetite? Why are not the worlds of appetite and abstraction in harmony? In other words, why does it so rarely happen that a web will remain undisturbed after its completion until it has yielded wisdom to the weaver? Ideally, a fly should land only after that golden moment. This happens by chance every now and again but it is really quite rare. Imagine how wise all arachnids could be!

"'Perhaps, however, we are not meant to know more than we should. There is a popular horror story told amongst us of a certain spider who tried a most unusual experiment. He decided to construct three webs in a row. He built the outside ones first and the inside one last. The outside webs sheltered the inside one. The webs to the front and back of the inside web stopped all flies coming in from both directions. The central web remained undisturbed. He could contemplate on it for as long as he pleased. He sat on the corner of the inside web and studied the fascinating weave at his leisure. He sat for hours and hours and great mysteries were gradually revealed to him. The wonders that the web disclosed, however, trapped him just as surely as webs entangle flies.

"'He was so totally consumed by the outpouring of knowing that he forgot himself. He forgot that he was a spider. He forgot that he had eight legs and a breast full of filament. All the knowing of himself vaporized. Just as he thought he was about to crack the riddle of the universe, a swallow came by and plucked him from his reveries.

"'I can never forget that story. Sometimes I think that webs are unnatural. If knowing can only come intermittently, then webs are illusions. This artform generates a false sense of completion. In truth, knowing is not so neat and compartmental. Knowing is more like dew. It is everywhere but it only gathers in little drops that plop off boughs one by one. Yet webs are not altogether deceptive. After all, they elevate the act of survival. Somehow webs prevent life from degenerating into ugliness.'"

There was a long silence. Mr. Severman had read the story with such strong emotion that both Mimi and Megwadesk had been carried away by the rhythms of his voice. Mimi and Megwadesk had expected another amusing story much like the stories Mr. Severman usually told about Pastor Duncan and his parish. The story about the spider left them speechless. Neither wanted to comment on it, each fearing they may have misunderstood it.

Megwadesk was most struck by the fate of the spider.

Nisgam! I've let myself make the same mistake the spider made, he told himself. *He let his mind get lost in all kinds of thoughts, eh - too many thoughts and nothing 'tall else but thoughts! Boys oh boys, I better get on with doing things before fate plucks me from my worries! Yep, I better check Skoltch's net tonight, for sure! This time, eh, I'll do it!*

What struck Mimi was the manner in which Mr. Severman had read. Something about the rhythms and emotions, had shifted her attention from the story itself to Mr. Severman. She knew that something was wrong. Mr. Severman's expression was melancholy.

"I should have followed my heart when I was young," he said, his eyes staring at something fading away.

"I try to follow my heart," Megwadesk said. "I think that's

good." That was all he could think to add. But he wondered, *Does Mr. Severman like stories more than his Christian beliefs? But how can a preacher feel that way? Me, I'm thinking our stories are just silly, eh, and I'm thinking maybe the Christian way is right but he's thinking maybe stories are what he should be telling.*

Mr. Severman smiled and said, "Yes. You have a great heart, my friend – too great for me to be wearing it out with stories that don't bring laughter. And, to tell you the truth, I'm somewhat embarrassed now to have read that piece to you. But what did you think of it? No, no! Don't bother answering! I read it to you because I desperately needed somebody to hear it. But did you find something striking in the story? No, never mind. No, I really should be along!"

"You sure you don't want another cup of tea before you go?" Mimi asked.

"No, thank you, Mimi. It's going to be dark soon. I must go. I'm afraid I don't have your husband's skill when it comes to navigating in the dark. I tried it once and ploughed right into a sandbar! I snapped an excellent keel and got a good bump on the head for my vanity! I learned my lesson, I tell you!"

They laughed.

"You don't have to worry about tonight, eh," Megwadesk said. "The moon'll be bright."

"Yes, but will it be clear or cloudy, hmm? And will there be sufficient wind? No, I really must go. I was tacking to windward on my way up here, and I certainly had fun jumping seats but, oh, I sure hope I won't be running with the wind on the way back. Give me a good broadside breeze any day! Well, I thank you both for your hospitality. You must visit soon and meet the missus. She will be so pleased to see you."

Mr. Severman put on his hat and then he pulled his jacket off the spike, unintentionally grabbing Megwadesk's jacket as well. Mr. Severman turned Megwadesk's jacket right-side-out and set it back on the spike.

When he saw the rip, he exclaimed, "My! What happened to this good jacket of yours?"

"Oh, working in the woods," Megwadesk mumbled.

Mimi examined Megwadesk's expression.

"You really should have this mended," Mr. Severman said, poking four fingers into the torn seam. He withdrew his hand and smiled, putting his black jacket on, and said, "Good-night, then!"

Megwadesk shook his hand and wished him good-night. When he felt Megwadesk's thickly calloused hands, Mr. Severman could not help but feel self-conscious about his hands, which he thought were too soft in comparison. Mimi got up and shook his hand and wished him good-night also.

Megwadesk added, "It was a good talk, Mr. Severman. Come again and visit soon."

"Yes," Mr. Severman murmured, stroking the short hairs on his nape as he stared at the threshold. Suddenly, without looking up, he asked, "My friend, do you sometimes wonder where God went?"

"Er, yes, sometimes," Megwadesk replied.

"Do you know what I sometimes think happened to God?"

"No, Mr. Severman."

"The same thing that happened to Humpty Dumpty."

Mr. Severman stared seriously into Megwadesk's eyes for a moment. Then he laughed. A bitter laugh. He recited, "And all the king's horses and all the king's men. . . . Well, good-bye."

The preacher waved as he hastened across the clearing. Megwadesk closed the door. He turned his head and saw Mimi staring at him.

"I don't think poor Mr. Severman's happy 'bout being a preacher," Megwadesk said.

"I got something like that feeling, too," Mimi said. "But I think he's grieving about something else he lost, like something he had a chance at once. Anyway, tell me – how did your jacket really get ripped?" she asked.

"I guess I forgot to mention Skoltch's dog 'tacked me this morning," he answered.

"Oh, my God! That dog ought to be shot! Were you hurt? Where did it bite you?"

Megwadesk unbuttoned his left cuff and rolled up the sleeve.

Mimi felt the arm.

"It's bruised and a little swollen but there's no cuts, thank goodness. Oh, yes, there's one, a hole, near the elbow. Does it hurt?"

"Hardly. I rolled my jacket 'round my arm and used it as padding, eh."

"Let me see your jacket."

"Well, I guess I've been expecting something like this for a long time, eh," Megwadesk said with a sardonic grin.

"What do you mean?" Mimi asked, studying the rip on the jacket.

After his reassuring conversation with Mr. Severman, every word of which he was sure Mimi had heard, Megwadesk thought he could now make light of his dreams.

"Well, for the past six nights now I've dreamt of animals 'tacking me, eh. I should've expected it to happen sooner or later."

Mimi released the jacket sleeve and stared at Megwadesk. "Cats? Horses?" she asked.

"Oh, yeah, 'n' bears, too," Megwadesk answered nonchalantly.

"Somebody's working a hex on you and you don't tell me?" Mimi asked, her voice lowered in anger. "I'll bet any money it's that witch, Old Molly! I warned you that she'd try to get at me through you!"

"Nisgam! After what Mr. Severman 'n' I just talked 'bout 'n' you talk like that?" responded Megwadesk. "It's just no use!"

Mimi seized a knife and the pouch of tobacco from the table, and then flung open the door and stomped outside. Megwadesk watched her sprinkle tobacco over the greenery in the front clearing and then cut off about a dozen large plantain leaves. From the river he heard the mast fall into its grooves with a loud thud. Then he heard the splashing of an inexperienced rower.

Long shadows stretched from the woods, leaving only Mimi's saffron back brightened by the light. The sun had yet to set but the pale moon was already scouting above the east in advance of the night. Mimi marched to the bushes, stalked in front of them like a drill sergeant inspecting troops, and then shook her head and disappeared into the woods. The sound of the splashing oars stopped. A few loud snaps followed as the sail was raised and then it became quiet.

Mimi returned from the woods. She had a branch in her hand. Megwadesk recognized the leaves. The bush was used for making magical weapons.

Mimi walked into the house. She set the branch on the sewing table and cleaned the plantain leaves in a basin of water. Then she removed one cloth diaper from the shelf. She tore the diaper into several strips.

"Reach out with your arm," she told Megwadesk.

Megwadesk reached out while he watched Mr. Severman's sailboat, a modest sloop, coast past the cove. Megwadesk noted that Mr. Severman had his wish: the wind was broadside.

"No," Mimi decided. "First, you might as well take off that good shirt. You won't need it again for a couple months."

Megwadesk removed his shirt. Mimi placed the plantain leaves over the puncture and around the area below the elbow and then bandaged the arm.

"This will draw out any infection," she said. Then she added, "And anything else that's bad, too."

"Anything else bad, huh," Megwadesk repeated sarcastically.

Mimi ignored his attitude and went to the sewing table and took the branch and knife. She cut off the leafy end of the branch and left a stalk about eight inches long in her hand. She started sharpening the ends.

"You'll sleep with this tonight," she told Megwadesk.

"Nisgam! How can you take nonsense like that seriously, eh, after what Mr. Severman told us?" Megwadesk shouted. "Boys oh boys, bana, I don't understand you! You heard everything he just told us! All them old beliefs are just superstitions an' now, here you are, running 'round sharpening that stick!"

"Just do it for me, okay!" Mimi shouted back. "Just keep it with you wherever you go and, when you sleep, have it handy."

"But how can you believe in this preacher 'n' believe in superstition at the same time, eh? You pray every day, so you must be Christian, an' still you let that old stuff make you crazy."

"What I'd like to know is, how can he believe in his religion and not believe in our ways at the same time? If a virgin can have a baby, then what's so crazy about our so-called superstitions? Nisgam! If our beliefs aren't true, then his can't be true either. He just doesn't want to believe in our ways and that's why he makes fun of us. And besides, you guys purposely picked the worst examples for your talk! Ha! You used characters we use in stories told for children! That's as bad as if I said I don't believe in Christ or God any more because Santa Claus doesn't exist! Why didn't you mention elísasid, the spirit we see when somebody close to us is about to die? People have seen *that*, haven't they! Me, I don't care what the preacher thinks. All I want to hear from him is, 'You are husband and wife.'"

Megwadesk felt like a fool. He did not know how he could have missed it all along. Perhaps he was too obsessed with the thought it had to be either one or the other. Mimi, he realized, was absolutely right. If Christianity was true then so, too, were their old beliefs. Both were dependent on things normally considered impossible. Then it occurred to him to take the thought even further, where Mimi had not dared to take it.

If, he told himself, *our old beliefs are just superstitions, then Christianity is just a superstition, too.*

And this thought slowly spread a smile across his mouth for he felt he had outstripped Mimi in her logic.

"So you don't believe me?" Mimi said. "Okay. Grin all you like! I don't care. Just promise me you'll keep this near you tonight. I tell you, you're not going anywhere until you promise me!"

Mimi walked to the quill-basket, that contained her sacred stones, and opened it. One of the rocks had been split and some of the amethyst crystals were loose. She took a piece of crystal and tied it to the end of the stick that she had sharpened on both ends and then she gave the stick to Megwadesk. Mimi removed the crucifix that hung around her neck and put it around his neck. Megwadesk went along with the whole ritual just to humour Mimi.

"Remember," said Mimi, "never let any animal that attacks you in your dream bite you! Remember your weapon! Reach for it in your dream and you'll find it!"

"I'll remember," Megwadesk answered, but his mind was already on another matter.

There was no doubt in his mind now that both witchery and Christianity were superstitions and this exhilarated him. Suddenly there was nothing to fear, nothing to inhibit him. He had neither retribution nor judgement to dread. The way was open for him to take whatever he liked from Skoltch's net. Why not? He reasoned that, if he cleaned the net of bass while Skoltch was snoring, the net was sure to be instantly refilled with more bass anyway. Skoltch would not miss a thing. It would not really be stealing, he reassured himself. Skoltch would still get his usual netful.

He congratulated himself, thinking, *It's a good thing I lied to Mimi, eh. She won't be expecting me to spear eels tonight 'n' tomorrow I'll be selling bass.*

Mimi told him, "I'm not mending your jacket. Why are you grinning? If you're going to hide something from me, then it's your business to take care of it."

Mimi helped him out of the rest of his good clothes.

"Honest to God," Mimi muttered, "I don't know where you would be without me."

Chapter Ten

Judgement Day

It was a bright night, just as he told Mr. Severman it would be. Although the moon was luminous, Megwadesk still had a small fire going, to keep the flies away – and, also, to see what he was doing. Mimi placed in his hand one last item before he left the house: a needle with a long piece of thread looped through its eye. Megwadesk sat on the flat stump by the river squinting at the seam, carefully mending the tear, and occasionally cursing Skoltch's dog. The seam slowly closed. But that was only half the job. He had to rethread the inside lining he had opened to get at the outside rip. Thousands of frogs sang from the swampy inlet to the east.

Megwadesk felt drowsy. He got up from the stump and sat farther away from the heat, hoping the cool night air would revive him. He had to hunch over to get enough light to see what he was doing. The lack of replenishing sleep for the past six nights and the lack of wholesome food in the past two days, more than the strenuous work of clearing a road, sent the occasional puff of exhaustion through his body and mind. What little sleep he got was not restful because he did not sink into the darkness that was deeper than dreams. His head throbbed. When he finally closed the inside lining, his eyes felt strained. He set the jacket on the stump. Megwadesk wanted to lie down and rest but he forced himself to his legs and walked to his boat.

On the bank between raspberry bushes and a cluster of small fir trees was the path to the shore. A magnificent spider web, large and gleaming and almost perfectly circular in design, was strung waist-high between the bushes and the fir. Megwadesk stopped just as he was about to plough

through it. The near perfect symmetry of the web astonished him.

What a wonderful weaver of nets, he thought.

He admired the web for a second and then he went
around it, going through the stunted firs. He had to push
the boat with rollers and poles to get it off the muddy shore
because the tide had dropped.

He set out to clean Skoltch's net. Even a very lucky net
would not catch a thing, if it was covered with slime and
moss. Now that he was determined to steal from Skoltch's
net, he had to make sure the net had every possible chance
of success. He couldn't afford to remove it and dry it out
and give it a thorough cleaning, but he could still pull most
of the filth off while it was still set. It was a messy job, cleaning a net while it remained in the water, and he did not look
forward to it.

He could now say with certainty that Old Molly had been
"foiling" him – or attempting to. Now that it was all superstition, it made no difference to him. He no longer had to
repress his suspicions. His instinct had told him all along
that Old Molly had something against him. Although her
hatred coinciding with his bad luck was a pure fluke – and
was not the cause of it – he still felt very pleased thinking
about avenging himself on those who wished him ill.

In the clear view of moonlight, he rowed around his net
to get to Skoltch's net. There were some sticks and wet
branches in his boat. He decided that, if anybody asked him
what he was up to, he would say he was cleaning Skoltch's
net and he would produce the sticks and branches as proof.
His new-found boldness surprised him. He did not even
worry about getting caught. This indifference, that gave him
such a sense of detachment, was a mildly pleasant experience to him. He thought if Skoltch caught him and asked
him what he was doing with the net, he would have
shrugged and said, "Just getting some sticks off," and there
would be no nervousness in his voice. As he got closer to
Skoltch's net, however, he began to lose some of his daring.

He thought, *I know there's no punishment I gotta fear, eh,
none from God's heaven or from the hell of witchery, then why'm
I hesitating?*

He stopped rowing and the tide started to pull him away

from Skoltch's net. His head pounded painfully.

It's the law, yes, that's it! That's what's got me all worried now, he thought. *Éq! I don't fear the laws of angels or demons, 'cause they're just imaginations – so why, eh, should I fear man-made laws? But, Nisgam, I'm not afraid! I'm just being thoughtful and cautious is all. Mustn't do nothing stupid – that's all. Damn, my head aches!*

He knew that stealing from a net was something his people condemned. A person could get badly beaten for it.

Steal? What'm I thinking? I'm not gonna steal. I just wanna be sure it's clean. But no, no. I won't look at it now. Later, he thought. *Yes, I'll come back 'n' look at it later. Besides, it looks clean from here, eh. The top line don't have filth on it like it did earlier today. Yes, I see what happened! Skoltch returned from Trenton an' cleaned it while Mimi 'n' I were feasting Mr. Severman. Éq, Nisgam! That net's perfectly clean! Oh, yes! I don't have to worry about it 'tall!*

Megwadesk gladly turned his boat around and rowed back to his net. He examined his net until he was satisfied everything was correct. Then he rowed to shore. He stretched his back on the deck for a few minutes. He wondered if his fatigue were due to lack of filling meals. He hadn't eaten much the whole day. A meteorite sparkled and went out. He stared at the moon and the clouds and then he closed his eyes.

He woke with a start. He caught himself just as he was about to roll off the deck. He groaned and looked up at the moon. It had hardly moved.

Nisgam! I fell asleep that fast? he wondered. *An' what a crazy dream I had!*

The forest still whistled with the singing of frogs. From upriver came the occasional bellow of a bull. Megwadesk saw the ghostly shape of a small sailing craft slowly drifting downstream. Apparently there was enough breeze out on the open water to blow up a sail but on the shore, so close to the tall pines, there was hardly a stir.

He had dreamt there was a storm but instead of blinding white lightning, the flashes were jagged black rods. Then the dull clouds parted and an enormous round body of a spider appeared. The black rods of lightning turned out to be the legs of the gigantic spider scuttling towards him.

Beside the spider was a snarling dog. The giant spider and the wild dog raced over where the river used to be, which had turned into a great open meadow. The gigantic spider had a human face but the face kept changing. At one point, it looked like Mr. Severman. Another time it looked like Skoltch. And then again it looked like a composite of Rancid and Father Colérique.

The spider saw Megwadesk and yelled, "There he is! He's got it! Get, boy! Get! Fetch it from him! Bring it back!"

Megwadesk ran up the hill to his house. When he reached the trail cutting through the woods, he saw a net made of thick thread blocking his path. He took his knife out of its sheath with his right hand and grabbed the net with his left hand, intending to cut through his way. When he touched the net, his fingers got stuck to it. A powerful glue-like substance coated the net. He looked up and saw the net stretching far up into the remaining clouds and beyond. He tried to pull himself free but he could not. He heard the dog's racing feet behind him, its hard nails scratching on stones with each great bound.

Megwadesk remembered Mimi's warning to make sure no animal bit him, so he glanced around for the stick she gave him. He could not find it. He felt his pockets with his free hand and realized he was carrying something the spider wanted. Nervously he tried to get it out of his pocket but each time he reached for it in one pocket, the thing disappeared and reappeared in another pocket. Then the dog leaped to his throat and knocked him back, and that was when he woke up.

Megwadesk could not believe how scared he had been in the dream. Now that he was awake, the dream struck him as outrageous, silly, even comic. Nevertheless, he wondered what he had done with the stick Mimi gave him. He threw the anchor on the grassy bank, which was a good throw for the tide was low, and then he got out of the boat. He saw something glowing white on the mud. He picked it up. It was one of the two dice he had thrown away the previous night. He put it in his pocket and walked to the stump, breaking through the web between the raspberry bushes and the fir.

Under his folded jacket, beside his clay-pipe and tobacco

pouch, was the little stick sharpened on both ends with the crystal tied to it at one end. He placed the dream-weapon in the hood of his jacket and put on the jacket. That way, when he fell asleep, his weapon would be handy – *just in case,* he told himself. He smoked a pipeful of tobacco-and-willow-bark mixture, hoping the tobacco would silence his growling stomach. As he smoked, he felt something in the jacket's left pocket. He reached into his pocket and pulled out a jar of pickled babycorn.

"Oquetédud!" he exclaimed joyfully. "Hey, now I've got something to munch on!"

He put out his pipe and opened the jar. He devoured all the pickled corn and licked his fingers clean before he screwed the lid back on the glass jar and set the jar on the stump. Laying down on his left side, he reached over with a stick and lazily brushed together the loose ends of the fire and tossed the stick into the renewed flames. His hands went over his head and twisted at the wrists as an ungovernable yawn pulled his jaws wide. His spine crackled and he rolled onto his back with a stretch, one stiffened leg off the ground and the other bent sharply at the knee.

A wonderfully slack sensation came in the wake of his contortions. He mentally relived a part of his day's activities – digging clams, making a fire, eating by the river – and he visualized this as if he were viewing himself from the air. Only the sound of the high winds accompanied these images – the same sad winds of time, he thought, that would blow long after his generation was dust. He did not know why he so frequently took that distant perspective whenever he reviewed each day's activities, except that it made him feel a consoling touch of self-pity. He seemed so small, so alone, so insignificant, so much like a child going about his business, which was nothing at all – nothing next to the river, the forest and the sky. Sometimes he felt that he would always be like a child and that even the greatest of men had been nothing more than children, too. What did a child teach another child? And he remembered his sister, Tiara, and himself and how they liked to play on the shore when all their work was done. Again he fell asleep.

This time, when he woke up, it was completely dark. He wondered if his fire had gone out. *It must've clouded over, too,* he thought. He stood up and stumbled around. *Boys oh boys, I must've slept a long time.* He groped around for the stump. It should have been to his right. Instead, he stumbled into bushes. Since he couldn't see anything, he listened for the water.

The lapping wavelets sounded farther away than they should have. He walked towards the sound of the water. Something told him to stop. He stood stock still, in the grip of an inexplicable fear, as if everything hung in the balance. Eventually he understood what was wrong. The sound of the water came from a distance below. When his eyes became accustomed to the gloom, he saw that he was standing only a yard from the edge of a forty feet high cliff. His boat was grinding against the rocky shore below. Suddenly he understood what had happened.

He had fallen asleep on his boat and had drifted to the cliffs a mile-and-a-half downriver from where he had been. What had happened? He remembered he had first checked his net. Then he rested on the deck for a bit. That was when he had fallen asleep. He must have only dreamt of everything else that followed. He dreamt that he woke up from his dream about the spider; he dreamt of throwing the anchor in the grass. He had not really gone to shore to smoke his pipe and to eat the jarful of corn. All that had been a dream, too, he reasoned. Because he had not placed the anchor in the grass, he ended up drifting to these cliffs while asleep on the deck. Then, no doubt, he had sleep-walked up the cliff. He used to do that often as a boy – sleep-walk, that is, he reminded himself. The sensation of waking up in a strange place came back to him as rich as the scent of childhood springtime grassfires.

It's funny, he thought. *It's been a long time since I last dreamed within a dream.*

Normally he would have asked himself how it was that the retreating tide had not left him beached, but accounting for what had happened was paramount on his mind and any likely explanation was so welcome that he could not trouble himself with scrutiny for, on a deeper level, the part that governed his equilibrium was aware that an explanation staved off the hidden but lurking notion he was experiencing something impossible, therefore something insane.

He followed a trail down the cliff and boarded his boat. He pushed it off and then jumped in. He was anxious to get back to his net but instead of taking to the oars, he stood on the deck and began poling. He wished he could see into the shallows. He sensed there were numerous fish streaming through the dark waters. He felt things bumping into his pole. The next instant, the sky opened and moonlight flooded down.

Megwadesk was amazed by the number of eels he saw streaming through the shallows.

"Boys," he said, "the river sure cleared up fast!"

Some eels slithered over the bottom. Others darted ahead, leaving lines of stirred mud in their wake. Still others trembled past just below the soft wavelets. The eels streamed around his boat, meeting as one body again just a few feet in front of the deck. There were so many they could not help bumping into his pole. Megwadesk saw himself as a man watching all his money blowing away in a strong wind. Were it not for the pole keeping his body upright, he would have slumped on the deck, devastated by the despair of not having his eel-spear with him. The school seemed to go on for hours.

It was a long time before he noticed he was no longer poling. He merely drifted with the rising tide. The tide carried him along upriver towards his net. He felt that he was going to the source of something other than the river, but what that source was kept escaping him.

Several times out of frustration, Megwadesk struck at the eels with his pole, hoping to knock one unconscious. At other times he tried to slap one from near the surface and into his boat. Nothing worked. Eels were tough. It was hard enough to hold onto one, even with a spear.

His mouth and lips felt dry. He kept licking his lips and swallowing his spit. His thirst became stronger. He wondered if he had really eaten the pickled babycorn. Their sour juices could account for his thirst.

Eventually the school thinned out and then there were no fish at all to be seen. Not even grubs. No doubt, eels had devoured every last grub and needle-back that went before them, he concluded. If it were not for the occasional bed of oysters and the seaweeds all stretching one way towards the source of the river, Megwadesk would have sworn he was staring into a dead lake. Nothing, not even a crab, stirred.

He drifted this way, gazing into the underwater limbo, for an unaccounted stretch of time. He let the tide carry him along, his only contribution being to periodically veer away from sandbars. Sometimes, especially when he stopped scanning the water and he let his eyes fix on one spot for too long, he saw visions on the muddy river bottom. The shadows of the waves became ravens flying in the dusk. Then the wings of the ravens became eyebrows and faces appeared. One of the faces became Talon and the shadows of the waves turned to dark prison bars over his face. Megwadesk shook the visions off by glancing away. So long as his eyes incessantly roved over the river bottom, no visions appeared.

He heard the water draining into river. He wondered if there was a moose wading in the river, draining its bladder. He remembered using his moose-call as a funnel and pouring water through it to duplicate this sound during their mating season. The sound came from his left. He poled towards it. It turned out to be a fount of spring water spouting from a mossy sandstone cliff! This was where he saw the doe and her fawn the night before. He realized he was just across from where his net was set. He looked across the river and saw the fire still burning. The high water made it possible for him to drink from the wonderful, refreshing spring without disembarking from his boat. He drank gallons, it seemed. He felt revived, strengthened. He rowed across the channel. Then he poled again over the shallows on the other side.

As he drifted closer to his net, something off to his left, very close to the channel, caught his eye. When he focused on it, he thought it was a human body sprawled out underwater. He looked away. He believed he was only seeing things. When he took another glance at it, the body was still there. It was not a hallucination. This scared him. The brilliant moonlight distinctly outlined a human form. It had to be a drowning victim. Because he had not heard of anybody in Messkíg drowning, he thought it was somebody from a neighbouring community. A good tide could carry a body here from as far away as Trenton.

He almost poled to shore. Just the idea of seeing a bloated corpse underwater on a night like this – or on any night, for that matter – terrified him. Chills ran consecutively and uncontrollably up and down his spine and he could feel the hairs on his nape bristle. But then, hoping the lifeless eyes would be closed, he began poling to the body. After all, he figured, if he did not pull it out immediately it might just drift away with the outgoing tide and it could be lost for many days. He would not like it if a Micmac body were left to feed the fish, so he figured white people probably felt the same way about their dead.

"Mnduágig!" he cussed. "If it's a drowning victim, eh, its eyes'll be open, for sure!"

Nothing was more ghoulish than looking into a pair of human eyes bereft of a soul. They seemed to devour the onlookers own soul. Megwadesk had seen that, at the moment of death, some individual's pupils dilated to the point of flooding the entire darks of the eyes, and it looked like the eyes had burst wide open from within themselves and the vacancy in eyes was a deep, dry well that echoed only one word: "Death, death, death."

Megwadesk, nevertheless, continued poling towards the body. His ribs ached from the stress of his breathing. His chest muscles felt like they were being pulled in two directions at once. He tried to breathe deeply but his nerves kept his stomach and lungs constricted.

As he got close to the body, he saw that its arms were swaying loosely in the tide, for it was very close to the channel. He also noticed a great school of striped bass, swinging in from out of the blackness of the deep and then, when they came near the body, suddenly veering off their usual course towards the shallows and sweeping back out into the channel to avoid the body. Seeing so many bass made him think of his net. He glanced up. His boat was parallel to his net. He glanced at the shore and he saw somebody sleeping beside the fire. He wanted to call him for help with the dead body, but he found that he was speechless. He could not voice a sound. He figured his fear had strangled him. He returned his attention to the body.

Dripping sweat glazed his vision. At this point, all he

could distinguish about the body was how it lay. Its feet were to the right of the deck. Its head, angled slightly downriver, leaned towards the channel. It appeared there were thick bunches of seaweed stuck to the body, waving in the water. When he realized the corpse was submerged only a few inches below the surface, and not sunk to the river bottom, he sensed that something was seriously wrong with the picture. A dead body, lying almost perfectly sidelong to the tide stream, should have already drifted past his net, even past Skoltch's net, in the fast incoming tide. Why had not this body moved?

It got snagged! It's stuck to something under it, eh! Could be a stake underwater! That's it! Megwadesk thought, relieved to find a rational answer before his imagination ran away with him.

He had to get almost right over the body before the distortions caused by the waves were decreased enough by the angle of vision for him to make out a pair of green-and-black leather boots. Looking up at the rest of the body he was, at first, relieved to see it was not face up. At the same moment, he realized it was a woman. Her long red skirts swayed in the water. She wore a red-and-green blouse. Her hair was grey.

Then an alarm so electrifying that it almost stopped his heart made Megwadesk tremble from head to toe. It was Old Molly in the water!

It was Old Molly and she was not dead! She was swimming just below the surface of the water and in her left hand were thorn shoots painted a brilliant crimson and bound together to form a switch! Her arms were not swaying lifelessly! She was actively lashing at the incoming school of striped bass, forcing them to veer away from Megwadesk's net and to re-enter the shallows just in front of Skoltch's net! Hovering around her and twisting around her body were dozens of lampreys – not seaweed!

Megwadesk was numbed to the point of thoughtlessness. He let his pole drop with a loud thud inside the boat. Instantly, the lampreys sprang away from her body, startled! Old Molly wheeled around underwater and glared at Megwadesk.

The outrage in her cold grey left eye was not comparable

to anything else Megwadesk had ever seen. Her right eye remained shut, the right side of her face twisted into knots of damaged nerves and muscles. The waves made her face swell and shrink and swell again. Her feral eye seemed to bulge out beyond proportion. And the shadows of the waves streaming over her face created in Megwadesk the sensation she was ascending over branch after branch, growing taller. Megwadesk spun around.

His impulse was to abandon his boat – just jump into the water and get the hell to shore as fast as he could! The lampreys seemed to read his intentions and they surged around his boat! But the moment Megwadesk turned around, he saw the man in white standing on the shore, just below the fire, looking at him. It was the same mysterious figure he had seen over a month ago. The man told him something but Old Molly's hand, splashing out of the water behind him, drowned out the words. Old Molly's hand slapped against the deck of the boat, her fingernails scraping it to get a firm grip. His impulse was to run but he found he could not move his feet. And then another hand struck the deck. The thorns lashed his pants. The lash sent a shock through his body. He had felt a similar sensation when Talon had almost knocked him out once in a sparring match. His arms dropped and his eyes glazed as the shock surged up his spine and then, at the base of his neck, seemed to burst into all directions like a swarm of bees pouring out of a hive under attack. Megwadesk groaned helplessly.

He looked to the shore again, hoping to find the man in white, hoping that this mysterious figure could save him, but the man had vanished. Then a cold, soaked, bony hand seized his right ankle with the strength of a trap and like a snare it continued to tighten. In spite of his fear, he congratulated himself for wearing work boots, otherwise without the leather to protect him he was sure her long, hard nails would have dug to his bones.

Megwadesk's breathing was shallow and fast. His body trembled. He felt paralysed yet he managed to slowly, though only partially, turn around so that his left side was to his attacker.

Old Molly was half out of the water, grinning fiercely, blowing water out of her thin-lipped mouth and enlarged nostrils, one hand gripping his ankle and the other tenaciously holding onto to her crimson switches. Her dripping hair fell over parts of her face and her shoulders like a tattered old canvas tent after a tremendous downpour. She slid her tongue over her bared bottom teeth. Old Molly hooked one heel over the corner of the deck and heaved herself aboard.

Megwadesk knew that he should kick her head with his free foot and knock her back into the water but her face was hideous and the thought of touching it, even with his boot, sickened him. Old Molly, crouched on the deck, looked up at him and grinned. While steadily eyeing him, she put her hand up to her face and then reached into her mouth with one finger. She gagged and her chest heaved. She pulled her hand out and shut her mouth. Again her chest heaved and her stomach contracted, then the cheeks of her mouth bloated. She opened her mouth and extended her tongue out. Megwadesk sprang free from her grip with a jolt of sheer terror. Old Molly's tongue and mouth were coated with wriggling, thick, white maggots as long as earthworms! Megwadesk fell on the floor of the boat. His head almost hit a galvanized bucket. Old Molly slowly stood up. With her one open eye still blazing into his eyes, she pulled her repulsive tongue in, closed her mouth and swallowed the maggots, her throat swelling as she gulped them down.

"Judgement day's here, quicker than you figured, dear," Old Molly said.

Megwadesk felt like he had been thrown in the coldest ocean depths. He could hardly breathe. He was sure that he was hyperventilating. *Oh my God, she's playing with my fears!* he thought. *She's toying with me!* He rolled onto his stomach, intending to spring to his feet and break away from there, but his legs felt utterly powerless. He managed only to crawl. And the more he wished to get away, the less he could crawl until he was flat on his stomach, groaning.

The boat drifted into his net. Old Molly jumped down from the deck and walked over to him. She placed a boot on the back of his head and said, "They'll say he was a good man and a good fisherman. They'll say, dear, that they can't figure out how he ended up so badly tangled in his net. They'll say maybe he was drunk. He was upset that he wasn't catching a thing, so maybe he drank a bit before he went out that night. That's what they'll say. Isn't that what they said about Edward when he drowned, dear? Now give me your head!"

Megwadesk grabbed the handle of the galvanized pail. As Old Molly reached down to seize him by his hair, he swung the pail into the air and struck Old Molly on her mouth.

"Oh!" Old Molly moaned, her head snapping back and both of her hands flying up to cover her face. Her switches landed in the net. Both of her thin lips, top and bottom, were cut and blood poured down her chin.

Megwadesk broke the spell of paralysis. He sprang to his feet. Old Molly lost no time in recovering, either. She was about to attack Megwadesk, one of her hands raised as if to strike, when she realized that she didn't have her switches in her hand. She quickly scanned the floor of the boat and then she looked around the boat to see if they were floating on the water. Finally she spotted them, tangled in the net. While she disentangled her switches, Megwadesk jumped out of the boat and landed breast-deep in the water.

Instantly the lampreys swarmed around him. He waded to shore as fast as he could, beating the lampreys off with his arms. Behind him, he heard a splash. He glanced back and saw Old Molly swimming towards him just a few inches below the water, waving her switches in front of her. Megwadesk ran with all his might, his hips breaking out of the water, and then his thighs. He was completely out of the water before he realized that a lamprey eel was sucking the blood out of his back, near the kidneys. His shirt was loose, untucked, so he did not immediately see the lamprey, writhing under his shirt. It wasn't until he felt the bite that he realized what was on him. He took his knife and cut the lamprey's body off from its head. For a moment the fish's head, with the inside of its mouth lined by many tiny suction cups, remained stuck to his back, his blood spurting through it. Then he ripped off the head.

Old Molly burst out of the water. She was waist-deep. She spit and blew water out of her nose and then waded to shore, seaweed and river-moss lining her hair. Megwadesk did not run up the bank to reach the clearing where the fire still burned but ran along the shore instead until he was below the wooded area. He thought he would have a better chance if he hid in the shadows of the forest. At least he would not be out in the open, under the bright moonlight. Also he hoped to find a good solid chunk of wood to use in self-defense. To his surprise Old Molly did not race after him. Once she was on the shore, she started up the bank, straight towards the man that lay sleeping beside the fire.

Good thing that animal's going after 'nother prey! thought Megwadesk, but as he turned to enter the woods, he saw the man in white standing above him on the bank only a few meters away. Megwadesk was startled. The man wasn't dressed in white, as Megwadesk had supposed all along, but rather his naked body glowed white as if his skin was a lampshade and in his breast burned a bright light. A loin-cloth was all he wore. There was no doubt that he was an Indian, for his features were all clearly outlined and distinctively native. His eyes, however, glowed green like the eyes of animals in the dark when caught by beams of light.

"Go and defend your body, you fool!" the man in white shouted in Micmac. "She's going after your body while it's asleep and helpless!"

Megwadesk realized with a shock that it was his body lying near the fire. *Then who am I?* he wondered. *If that's my body there, eh, then what am I?*

"You are Megwadesk," the man in white told him, as if he had read his mind, "but the spirit and the body of yourself are separated. Go and help your body for, if she kills the body, then you will surely be dead to the earth!"

Megwadesk saw Old Molly running towards the body that lay asleep near the fire. In spite of the danger of the moment, Megwadesk found himself fascinated by what he saw. *Do I really look like that?* he wondered, amazed by his size. *Yes, that's me, eh, but I never thought, never imagined I had such a shape! I look bigger and stronger than I ever imagined!* These thoughts raced through his head as he sprinted towards Old Molly and his sleeping body. For a moment, he even felt a touch of vanity because his body – and especially the impression of physical strength it made – pleased him very much and suddenly he felt that it would be a terrible pity to see such a fine frame damaged or even destroyed and he became very eager to protect his body. He even wished he could see his body get up and walk around. *If it looks that strong while it's lying, I bet it looks really tough standing, eh,* he thought. He had seen his reflection in mirrors countless times before but seeing himself from outside his body created a totally different impression. Reflections were flat compared to the solidity of what he was seeing now.

"Reach behind you for your weapon," the man in white shouted after him. "Remember your weapon."

Megwadesk remembered placing the stick sharpened at both ends in the hood of his jacket. With a trembling hand, Megwadesk reached behind him and pulled the little stick out from the hood. When he had the stick in front of him, he was puzzled as to how he was supposed to use it. He wondered, *Do I stab with the crystal end or the bare end?* He saw Old Molly reach down to the sleeping body. He was about a hundred yards from her and fast shrinking the distance between them. It flashed across his head that Old Molly was going to strangle his body. *That's good,* he thought, *'cause then I got time to get to her before my body can be choked to death!* But the next instant, he saw Old Molly reach for the knife strapped to his sleeping body's waist. Just as Old Molly was about to grab the knife, she noticed the empty bottle of babycorn lying beside the body.

"You ate the corn?" she asked, with a bewildered expression, looking up at Megwadesk as he charged towards her.

"Yes, an' I'm gonna kill you now!" he shouted, raising the dream weapon.

Old Molly gasped when she saw the tiny stick with the crystal on it. Quickly she seized the knife, but she fumbled with the strap that went around the handle and held the knife in its sheath. The moment she touched the knife, however, the dream weapon that Megwadesk wielded sprouted from both ends. The stick stretched out to a ten feet long pole and the crystal expanded into an eel-spear of purple amethyst, complete with wired bracing at the base of the prongs. Megwadesk cupped the spear with an underhand grip and stared at it for a second, just as surprised as the old woman by the transformation.

Old Molly's left eye widened. Her right eye popped open. She caught her breath and let go of the knife. Then her right eye snapped shut and half her face involuntarily contorted into a grin. She sprang to her feet and immediately ran back into the water. Megwadesk raced after her until he was up to his waist in the water.

In her panic to escape, Old Molly almost dove headlong into the net. The lampreys jostled anxiously around her. Old Molly managed to swerve from the net just in time, releasing her switch to free both her hands to make a vigorous turn. She then wheeled around underwater and tried to free her switches from the net. In the meantime, Megwadesk decided to climb aboard his boat so that he could get a better aim at her. Once on deck, he assumed the posture of a spearthrower, the big toe of his left foot and his outstretched left arm in line to his target and his right arm, with the eel-spear balanced on it, poised over his head and just a bit to the back. Normally one did not assume such a dramatic poise when using an eel-spear but then again he was not spearing an eel. When Old Molly glanced up and saw him, she abandoned her switches and, as quick as an eel, darted out to the deep.

For a moment, Megwadesk was almost mesmerized by the graceful way Old Molly's body turned underwater. In one stroke she rolled over and had her back to him as she swam away from his boat, the lampreys streaming around her. The beguiling motion of her twisting body almost made his head spin.

Everything's upsidedown, he thought. *This is crazy!*

Just as she began her descent towards the channel, Megwadesk snapped out of his immobility and hurled the spear. He struck Old Molly through her left forearm. Megwadesk had to throw the spear because Old Molly had glided a good distance within that instant. The spear impaled Old Molly's arm into the muddy river bottom. The lampreys dispersed in all directions. She twisted to turn around and gaze from underwater. Both her eyes rolled; bubbles streamed out of her mouth. Then the right side of her face cramped into ridges and her right eye twitched and then closed. Megwadesk watched the end of the spear, sticking out of the water, tremble like a lance impacted into a wall of the hardest wood.

When Megwadesk looked to the shore, to make sure that

his body was fine, he saw a figure appear from the woods and stalk towards his body, the sleeping body that lay next to the fire. It was impossible to tell who it was, for it skulked close to the bushes and the shadows.

"Hey, you!" Megwadesk shouted, "What are you up to?"

But the figure appeared not hear him at all. It kept creeping up to his prone body, looking around every now and then. Several times the figure even looked out at the river towards where Megwadesk stood but the sneak acted as though he had not seen a thing out on the water. Megwadesk shouted at the shadowy shape again but it still did not seem to hear him. And then he realized, *Of course! If I'm in my dream form now 'n' he's in his real body, he can't see me! Old Molly must've been in his dream form, too, so I could fight her. But how can I defend my body 'gainst him, eh? I've gotta wake up 'fore it's too late! But how do I wake up, eh?*

He looked on helplessly as the dark shape raced up to his sleeping body. *I'm dead,* he thought, *I can't wake up!* But the stealthy figure merely scooped something up from the stump beside the sleeper and then raced silently up the hill, disappearing into the trail that cut through the woods and went up to his house.

Chapter Eleven

Power Reclaimed

A ball of resin in the fire beside him popped and sent large, flaky wafers of fire climbing into the air. They glowed and dimmed and glowed again like fire-flies. The flight of the sparks was a series of sudden vertical lifts followed by short horizontal slides so that to Megwadesk's awakening eyes the weightless embers seemed like they were mounting invisible stairways. And the stairways spiralled like mountain trails towards the Milky Way, the Spirit's Road. A shooting star sliced through the ascending embers.

His eyes opened wide and he hastily sat upright. The boat was still anchored to the grassy bank. It had all been a fantastic dream! Still, the unnerving essence of his vivid and eerie dream pervaded his surroundings.

He wanted to run away from the setting – from the shadowy woods, the moonlit river, and the growing fog by the inlet. He understood now what Talon had described when he told him, "I had this feeling, like I could make my dream real, like I could pull it into this world!" Some vague yet tangible thing from his dream lingered in the air and mingled with the dew, and it beckoned him to call the rest of it forth, to will the whole of its weirdness into this world. He forced his eyes away from the woods for fear of seeing the man in white standing in the shadows, peering intently at him.

No! Them things don't belong in this world, he thought, *'cause that would turn everything over!*

When he heard a commotion of splashing on the water, Megwadesk sprang to his feet, ready to bolt up the hill. He could visualize Old Molly bursting out of the water, yank-

129

ing the eel-spear off her bloody and clotting left forearm, and wading vigorously to shore, seaweed and river moss lining her hair! He looked at the river. The splashing grew more violent. He saw a wildly slapping hand break the surface and then splash back into the water! She was drowning! *Help her?* he asked. *No, flee while I can!*

He turned and was about to run, when he mentally replayed the image and discovered that, no, it had not been a hand but a fish, a bass! He turned to look at the river again and, yes, he confirmed it – striped bass caught near the surface of his net were jumping and splashing in an attempt to break through!

He was about to ride on a great wave of euphoria but then he cried, "Gisúlk! This is just what I saw in my dream, eh – bass trying to reach the shallows in front of my net!"

And it struck him that Old Molly must certainly be in the water close to the channel, pinned by the spear. It was her dreadful presence he had been feeling all along!

Without thinking what he was doing, he pulled the chain around his neck and cupped with both hands the tiny cross Mimi had given him. He rapidly prattled two *Hail Marys*, before his heart curbed its wild palpitations. He wiped the sweat off his entire face with the right sleeve of his jacket.

With a trembling hand he reached for the glass jar for he was thirsty. He opened the jar and drank the sour liquid, all the while keeping his eyes on his net. The extremely acrid taste of the liquid sent a shiver through his head and a needle into his brain, leaving no doubt at all that he was completely back in the bitter yet sweetly ordinary world. He drowned the entire contents and returned the jar on the stump. And that was when he noticed that his pipe was gone. Instantaneously he remembered seeing in his dream the shadowy figure run up to the stump and take something!

Could it be that I really was out of my body, eh? he asked himself. And quite suddenly, he had no doubt that he had seen accurately in his dream, for, when he studied the grass around the stump, he saw foot prints - very distinct, dull, flat prints against a carpet of glittering and silvery, dew-sprinkled turf – leading from the stump to the path that went to his house!

He thought, *Son of a gun! Boys oh boys, he can't be far!* He *might be at the house by now, eh! That's gotta be the guy Mimi told me 'bout! That must be him! An' he's likely to be peeping around the house now! But why didn't I see his footprints, eh, them other times I checked 'round the house after Mimi said he'd been 'round?*

Megwadesk ran up the trail. He felt both worried and extremely vigorous and capricious at once. He was concerned for Mimi's safety but at the same time he felt powerful, and this sense of power made him somewhat giddy, and he looked forward to testing his strength against the unknown prowler. His insides felt like they were bulging with invisible muscles. He felt like he could leap to the treetops. Whether he had actually speared the old witch, he did not know, but he was certain that, whatever it was he had done and whatever it was that had happened in his dream, it had all been to his benefit. His actions had corrected his path. The only thing he could compare this new sensation with was the feeling he had after he beat Rancid and he discovered the powers of an adult body. His new-found strength even made him feel very self-conscious and somewhat awkward, as if eyes were judging how he carried his added self. Again he had discovered another power in him, but this power was not entirely a physical one – even if it made him feel like he could kick the top of the tallest pine. And he thought he understood now how Talon had felt after he shot the deer that he had seen in his dream. He wondered, *Is this what magic feels like?*

It was easy to follow the footprints, and he could do so on a run, for the moon lent a sheen to the untrampled, dewy grass while the tracks came out dark like spots on a velvet surface where the hairs had been pulled against the grain. The footprints led directly to the house. Because he did not hear any commotion, his worries concerning Mimi's safety eased somewhat. He figured that the prowler had to be slinking around outside, probably looking for other items – tools perhaps – to steal. Then it occurred to him that it was very strange for the thief to have taken his pipe. *Why did he take such a chance?* he asked. *Why, he could've 'woken me - 'n' all for just a pipe! He must be stupid, eh!*

When he reached the clearing before the house, the front yard, he was amazed to find the figure standing off to the side of the house in clear view. The house was dark and Mimi was probably asleep, Megwadesk decided, but the moonlight was more than enough to clearly bring out the prowler's silhouette. Megwadesk stared at the figure and he was absolutely certain that the imposing figure was staring right back at him. Although Megwadesk could not see his eyes, the unmistakable angle of his head made it impossible for the grim shape not to see Megwadesk. The figure looked powerful, for he seemed to possess a huge frame, but Megwadesk, never for a moment, doubted his new-found strength.

No man 'round here's that big, he told himself, *so it's gotta be a spirit! Might be it's one of Old Molly's hellish friends! No matter to me 'tall, though, 'cause I'm ready!*

He did not feel the familiar combination of apprehension and anger that usually turned his stomach just before he got into a fight. Later, when he reflected on this, he found it strange, but at the time he only felt a peculiar joy. It was not a lust for violence, but an eagerness to try his powers. *Well, demon, let's grapple, then!* he thought. As Megwadesk walked towards the motionless figure, he realized that it wasn't such a big figure, after all. Nor was it a spirit. It was a man with bushes sticking up from his shoulders and head. The thick bushes had created an impression of great size.

Oddly enough, the realization that he was dealing with a man and not a spirit made Megwadesk a little uneasy. He was almost certain that the man was a lunatic. *He must be raving mad,* he thought, *'cause why else would he stand there looking so calm, staring at me, eh, 'n' acting like nothing, when I've caught'm red-handed creeping 'round my house?* The notion that he might have to battle a madman scared him because he had heard that maniacs had superhuman strength when they were enraged. Nevertheless, Megwadesk did not break his stride and soon he was almost up to the prowler's face. Still, Megwadesk did not recognize the prowler for his face was smeared with a dark substance.

"Hey! You can't see me!" the prowler said. It was Rancid! His voice was unmistakable. He sounded genuinely surprised that Megwadesk could see him, though why he should have assumed that he couldn't be seen when standing out in the open was something that astonished

Megwadesk.

"Well, I do see you, all right!" Megwadesk answered, his voice trembling with anger. *The idiot must be a Peeping Tom,*he thought.

"But you're not s'posed to see me!" Rancid said, stupidly blinking. "I'm s'posed to invisible like I was before!"

Megwadesk swore, "You son of a – "

But before he could even finish, Rancid was in full flight, tearing towards the trail that went to the cemetery. Megwadesk ran after him. Once in the woods, Megwadesk expected Rancid, being perfectly camouflaged, to veer away from the path and leap straight into the bushes in order to lose him. But Rancid – *like a fool,* thought Megwadesk - stayed on the trail, hoping to outrun his pursuer. *He's gotta be too scared to think straight, the creep!* concluded Megwadesk, *'cause I ain't the one all loaded down with bush, eh! Nothing's gonna slow me down!*

Megwadesk tackled Rancid to the ground just a short distance before the cemetery. Megwadesk dove to Rancid's waist and knocked him down but as both of them crashed into the earth, some of the branches attached to Rancid's back scratched Megwadesk's face, badly stinging his left eye. Although half-blinded by the tears streaming down his one eye, Megwadesk doggedly hung onto Rancid. He pulled himself up to Rancid's torso and then began to swing wildly at the back of Rancid's head, neck and shoulders. Rancid kept his face covered with his arms.

"Don't come creeping 'round my house again!" Megwadesk shouted. Rancid groaned. Megwadesk directed his punches lower and pounded Rancid's ribs and kidneys. Rancid rolled over and kicked back.

Megwadesk stood up and ordered Rancid to get up.

"You idiot," Megwadesk said, seizing Rancid by his throat, "what makes you think nobody can see you, anyway?"

"'Cause you never seen me before!" Rancid answered and he couldn't help but laugh and boast for a moment. "Ha! You walked right in front me so many times looking for my footprints! My godmother's gonna fix you! Let me go. . . I'm choking!"

Megwadesk wiped the tears from his eye and looked at

Rancid's chest and he saw his pipe strung to a necklace of sinew and thorn berries. He noticed again the little white squares painted on the stalks of the branches that were tied to Rancid. Megwadesk snapped the necklace off and took his pipe.

"Why you keep taking my pipe for, anyway?" he asked.

"Like it, that's all," Rancid answered, grinning.

Like it, like hell! Megwadesk thought. *You been using it 'gainst me, more like.*

Suddenly he punched Rancid on the chin. Rancid dropped to the ground.

"She won't be fixing anyone," Megwadesk told Rancid, "'cause I already fixed her."

Megwadesk was about to walk away but after taking three steps he stopped, turned around, and looked at Rancid and said, "If I ever catch you sneaking around my place 'gain, I'm gonna really hurt you bad."

Megwadesk walked back to the shore. When he got there, he saw his net trembling. *That's a welcome sight,* he thought, and he knew that bass were filling his net. He watched his net for a long time. His net filled up first and then the rest of the school went around his net and began hitting Skoltch's net. *This is how it should've been all along, eh,* he thought, *'cause I know the stream 'n' I know the shallows 'n' I knew I'd judged right. That's where the bass should've been swerving to shore all 'long.*

Megwadesk got into his boat and threw to shore the branches he had aboard. He poled to the shore-end of his net and then pulled himself along by the net a short distance until he got to the first bass. One after the other, hooking them by the gills, he flung the lively fish into his boat, and he frequently exclaimed, "Jumping Joseph, this is more than a ten pounder!"

Soon his hands were constellations of stars, coated as they were by glittering fish scales. His fingers and palms and nails – and even the pants over his thighs – glinted of fine scales like frost in the moonlight. He stretched his arms out and slowly turned his hands to see them glimmer. Then he noticed that many fire-flies were travelling along the shore creating a sparkling trail over the bushes.

He pulled more bass from his net. How he loved the

round button-eyes of bass – the even white rims on the out-
sides and the determined black plates in the centres! And
sometimes in the moonlight the depths of those dark centres flashed an iridescent steely blue! Now that he had been
forced to do without for some time, he felt his bond with
the fish magnified by his gratefulness, and the profound
respect the ancients had accorded each species made sense
to him. He loved the fish he caught because they came to
him. The way the fish never looked back at him but kept
their focus always elsewhere – in another world – spoke to
him of a complete lack of defiance, of a mysterious willingness to sacrifice for humans. Maybe willingness was not the
correct word. Perhaps they simply accepted their role. Then
it struck him that it was a shame his people no longer performed the ceremony for calling bass. Such a splendid creature deserved at least that much of a yearly tribute from the
people. And not just from the Micmacs, but from the French
and the English, too, and everyone else who fished for it.

He felt a hot blush of shame on his cheeks and on the
back of his neck, when he recalled how Talon had once
wanted to revive the ceremony for calling salmon and how
everyone in the meeting, except Skoltch, had laughed at him.

The chief's wife, decked out in the latest fashions and
her face heavily powdered, had been enraged, and had
yelled, "You want the people around here to think we're
still a bunch of backward savages, or what?"

When Talon had looked his way for support, Megwadesk
had quickly turned his head.

Skoltch had shouted, "My kin and friends, let us hear
him out!"

Then Talon had continued, declaring, "Amudj dagadu,
it's funny how in church they say give thanks to God for
everything. So I suppose instead of giving thanks to the
salmon we should all go to mass and give thanks to God *for*
the salmon. Isn't that so? Then how is it when Henry here
or Laleve there does us a favour, we don't thank God but
we go and thank Henry or Laleve instead? Sometimes only
afterwards do we thank God for what Henry or Laleve did.
Why? I'll tell you why. Because we're so special as
people we even have God all decked out just like one of
us, and what's true for us isn't true for the animals that keep

us alive!"

Very few people understood his point and some even loudly demanded to be told what Henry and Laleve had ever done for the community. Everybody sensed, though, that something blasphemous had been said and Talon had been forced to leave.

But before taking his leave, Talon had added, "I'm sure there are still Indians out there somewhere who are taking care of the earth, but when they die out you can be sure the fish will stop returning, for you and for everyone else!"

Megwadesk now understood what Talon had intended with the ceremony. He even felt guilty as he took the fish, for the fish were faithfully doing their part but he had not done his.

When he reached for another bass, he noticed something red stuck in the net. He raised the net out of the water and saw thorn shoots painted red and bound together to form a switch. He noticed that there were tiny white squares painted on the stalks. *These are the same marks Rancid had on his sticks,* he thought, *so – really? – can it be? – that Old Molly's magic, while she had power over me, made him invisible?* Instead of fear he felt the strength of his new-found powers of perception, and immediately he knew exactly what to do to cleanse his net of witchery completely.

He carefully removed the switch, so he would not make a single unlucky tear on his net, and rowed to shore. He jumped out of his boat with the switch, and walked up to the fire. He grabbed wood from the pile he had gathered earlier, made the fire strong, and then tossed the switch into the flames. The red thorn stalks sat in the crackling blaze, unaffected by the flames, as if they were cast from iron. Suddenly they blackened and then crumpled into ashes.

More splashing came from the river. The part of the net he had cleaned of bass began to vibrate as another school of bass sought to swim through it. He smiled and wondered how great his haul would be. Then he remembered the stone throwers. In the morning he would have to row past the bridge in Trenton. He would have to leave very early.

Chapter Twelve

One Last Test

The crate of food he lugged pulled his shoulder joints. He should have felt pain but he was beyond physical sensations now. His body was numb. His legs marched across the little clearing by the river and then up the hill in the same rigid pace. To slow down, to speed up – these things expended too much energy and he was strictly on automatic now. There were pins and needles on every square inch of his skin. What surprised him was that he no longer had a headache. He was just beat. He knew he had worked himself to the point where even two days of sleep would not recuperate him. He figured the whites of his eyes had to be thickly lined with veins.

Nope, no amount of sleep would help. Oh, but how he still yearned to sleep, though – to sleep, sleep, sleep! To snuggle up against Mimi and wrap his arms around her waist and doze off with his nose in her soft, forest-scented hair! He was sure he would have no more nightmares. And when he woke up, he would eat and eat!

No doubt, his battle with the buowinéskw had taken a great deal out of him. But even without the added spiritual stress, he had worked around the clock and denied himself enough sleep to accumulate the rest time of a dozen overworked men.

The euphoric energy he had gained after his battle with Old Molly had quickly dissipated but not before he had come to a realization. Rowing to Trenton, he kept replaying in his mind the battle with Old Molly. The outcome of the conflict had freed him from the oppressive sensation of powerlessness, of being a passive agent trapped in the designs of fate.

In the end, he saw that his thinking had misled him while his hunches, his intuition, which he had tried so hard to repress, had been correct. He understood that his salvation had not rested on doing anything dramatically out of character but, on the contrary, salvation had rested on remaining true to character, even in – indeed, especially in – the face of unfamiliar difficulties, those straits most predisposed to upset one's psychological poise. In his case, remaining true to his character entailed trusting his intuition, which had, after all, always been his ultimate instructor when it came to successful fishing. This realization came to him with the freshness and clarity of a wordless insight. It would be weeks before he would even attempt to tentatively express it in unsatisfactory terms to anyone.

He had rowed, with over three-hundred-and-fifty pounds of bass on board, all the way to Trenton and then back because the wind had died. He had taken his sail with him for he had hoped Wejúsyn would eventually beat its tremendous wings but it never did. When he finally got back, he tossed the anchor to shore, left his sail on the boat, left his centreboard under the deck, and left his net in the water. He would look after that stuff later.

He shuffled up the hill with the crate of food and heard Skoltch's rooster from the other hill crowing. Megwadesk had seen Skoltch near the bridge.

Megwadesk had been returning from having sold his catch and Skoltch had been on his way to sell his. A small group of young men on the bridge had been about to throw stones at Skoltch but when they seen another Micmac boat coming towards the bridge from the opposite side, they decided to retreat. Skoltch rowed off to the side to leave Megwadesk the entire channel. He stared wide-eyed at Megwadesk, scratched his elbow absently and, with his mouth hanging open, jerked his head once in a stiff and quick nod of greeting. Skoltch was unable to say a thing and instead, jabbed a cigarette in his mouth.

Megwadesk, gazing fixedly at Skoltch, answered with a deliberately slow nod, saying, "The weather is always better after a storm."

Suddenly Skoltch found his voice: "Is that spot we're set now going to be good much longer? My haul is pitiful."

Skoltch struck a match and lit his cigarette as Megwadesk answered.

"It'll be good for a few more days, then I'll have to find another," Megwadesk answered, stopping to rest.

Skoltch then shouted, the words rushing out like the smoke from his lungs, "Listen, Megwadesk, it wasn't my idea! I never liked the whole thing right from the start! I already warned her! But what could I do? If she won't listen, am I supposed to betray my mother?"

Megwadesk said, "Glúskeb found a village of Indians dying from thirst. Remember that story, Skoltch?"

"I tell you, it wasn't my fault! I warned her!"

"The river had run dry, Skoltch, so Glúskeb followed the dry bed 'til he found a huge dam made of skins woven together, like a gigantic bladder, eh. A boy, a servant, walked up to him 'n' he told the boy he was a man from the village. He asked the boy for a drink, eh, but the boy returned with muddy water. That was all the master would allow the boy to take to the stranger. Nothing else 'tall."

"Will you listen to me? I'm not responsible for what she does! I tell you, I tried!"

"So Glúskeb dashed the dish of muddy water on the stones, Skoltch, 'n' Glúskeb shouted, 'He's hoarding all this good water, yet he gives me this filth to drink?' He walked into the lodge of the master of the dam 'n' saw a huge man sitting inside, eh, his stomach all bloated up from drinking so much water 'n' his feet webbed from swimming around in it so much."

"Nisgam, I know the story already! I know! I know! You can stop now!"

"Glúskeb changed himself into a giant, Skoltch, 'cause Glúskeb had hidden powers that the greedy man didn't know nothing 'tall 'bout, eh. Glúskeb grabbed the greedy man 'n' broke his back over his knee, Skoltch. Then he squeezed him 'n' squeezed'm 'til most of the water was wrung from his body 'n' his skin was all wrinkled 'n' the man was shrunk to the size of your palm, Skoltch."

"You don't have to say the rest! Nisgam! I know!"

"Glúskeb told him, 'From now on your voice will always sound dry, for you will always thirst, 'n' your back will remain hunched. You'll no longer be a threat to the people.

139

They'll call you skoltch, frog!' Then Glúskeb set frog free."

Megwadesk laughed and said, "Go on! You're free, Skoltch. Go your way! Just don't set your net beside mine after I move it, eh!" And then he had laughed even harder.

Skoltch shouted, "You don't believe me, then? Well, go ahead and laugh! You go to hell! Every one of us is caught somewhere between good and evil, so don't you go acting like you're so good!" And Skoltch had thrown his cigarette into the water, seized his oars, and rowed away fuming, his infuriated eyes bulging.

Megwadesk chuckled at the memory of Skoltch's reddened face.

Skoltch had tugged his oars so strenuously that Megwadesk was sure if he had been carrying a heavier load, he would have snapped his oars. Foaming whirls spun from Skoltch's slicing blades and a parallel row of bubbles had issued from the corners of his transom. He had even created an impressive wake.

Megwadesk's laugh had a bitter edge to it. He despised Skoltch. Skoltch depended on him to find good fishing spots and yet Skoltch turned around and did *that*. Why, it was betrayal of the worst kind! Megwadesk despised Skoltch even more when he remembered Skoltch eagerly desiring to be his child's godfather. But this made him wonder, for Skoltch had been genuinely enthusiastic about becoming a godfather. Maybe Skoltch, after all, had played no part in the sinister scheme, he thought. Still, nothing could excuse his inaction. He could have at least warned Megwadesk. Or if he knew his mother was up to no good, then he should have set his net elsewhere, away from where Megwadesk had set his, so the evil would not have troubled Megwadesk. No, there was no excuse, Megwadesk concluded. Skoltch had been greedy. By doing nothing to warn Megwadesk, Skoltch had passively approved of the whole design. *Yes, Megwadesk thought, I am right to despise him.*

He reached the clearing in front of the house and saw two chubby women walking away, taking the trail through the woods that went past the cemetery and on to the main part of Messkíg. They were his mother and Mimi's mother. They disappeared into the woods, hooting loudly and chatting with vigorous gestures, happy and excited about something. When he entered the house, Mimi exclaimed and rushed up to him to take the heavy crate of food from him.

"Nisgam, Máli! So you *did* make a good deal! I thought you were kidding me! I expected to see you smoking your pipe by the window when I woke up!"

"Oh, no, this doesn't come from Skoltch's net. It's all mine, eh. One-hundred percent."

"Holy Moses! Your luck must be back!"

"Oh, it never left me. Somebody just put herself between myself 'n' it, that's all."

"What do you mean?" Mimi asked, her voice losing its lightness.

Megwadesk took her shoulders in his hands and said, "First you tell me what your visitors have hatched this time, eh."

Mimi smiled. She said, "Well, have a seat!"

"Oh, no! I fear that if I sit I won't be able to get up again."

"God, you look like it, too! Did you just tangle with the devil or what?"

Megwadesk chuckled, "You could say that. Now tell me about our mothers."

"Their plans even surprised me this time! But first they acted like they were just concerned about my condition. They took turns giving me all the old advice. 'Never get frightened by crippled or deformed people,' your mother said, 'or your child will be marked by these traits. If you scare easy, then don't make any journeys or meet any new people. Keep with your friends and relations.'

"Then my mum said, 'Yes, and don't get into any arguments and stay away from places where you might see fights or any violent accidents, if – that is – you don't want a testy baby!'"

Megwadesk smiled and asked, "Did they tell you never sit near a window, eh, if you want an easy time in labour?"

"Oh, yes! That, too! They covered all the bases. 'Don't deny yourself any food, dear,' they told me, 'even if you get a sudden craving for food you never cared for before!' And, 'Drink tea to calm yourself! We'll mix you some good herbal tea.' Meantime, I kept wondering, What are they really up to?"

"And what *were* they up to?"

"Turns out, your mum figured that chances were, we'd get Mr. Severman to marry us without problems. She says those preachers are always out to steal souls. Ha! Anyway, she decided to go see my mum first before coming here. The two of them sat down and planned out our wedding!"

"Ah ha! I thought it had to be something like that, eh. But that's good – isn't it? We can always use the help."

Megwadesk took his jacket off and hung it on the spike.

"But their plan doesn't include Mr. Severman!"

"No?"

"Not at all. They want the marriage to take place in Weladeg, during the St. Anne's Day celebrations. As you know, there's no priest living in Weladeg, but the bishop sends different priests to their church every so often – mostly on special occasions."

"Éhe, I know. He baptizes the children, blesses graves, hears confessions, celebrates Holy Communion, and – "

" – and marries couples!"

Megwadesk laughed and said, "That's right! But do you think people here are going to leave their celebrations to check out the celebrations at a smaller reserve?"

"They want us to go ahead, so we can talk to the priest as soon as he gets there and set the wedding on the last day of his stay there. That way all our relations from here can first celebrate St. Anne's festivities in Messkíg before going to Weladeg for our wedding."

"Isn't that like pulling one over on Father Colérique?"

"I guess so. But what your mum really hopes is that we talk the priest in Weladeg to stay until after the celebrations, so people here won't look like they're abandoning Father Colérique during the most important mass of the summer."

"And you like this plan?"

"I don't care how Father Colérique takes it. What I like is that everybody wants to chip in and help us. And, after all, I don't have anything against the priests who go to Weladeg. Besides, I thought all night about what your mother said. She made me so mad but, Nisgam, she was right!"

"What did she say?"

"Remember? She said that our child won't fit in if she is brought up in a different religion. And here I am, so mad about the hell I went through that I'm not even thinking straight. What do you think?"

"What will we tell Mr. Severman, though?"

There was a knock on the door. Mimi answered while Megwadesk put the food on the shelf. He heard a child's voice outside. It sounded familiar. He tried to place it.

"Sugar?" Mimi asked. "Sure. No problem at all, dear. How's your poor grandmother?"

The child mumbled something. Mimi said, "That's too bad! Give me the cup, then, dear."

Mimi walked to the dining table and was about to fill with sugar the cup the girl had given her, when Megwadesk sprang towards her and grabbed her wrists.

"Hold it!" he said, his eyes frantic.

"What's wrong?" Mimi asked, startled.

"Don't put anything in that cup! Here! Give it to me! I have to ask that girl something first!"

Megwadesk walked to the door and saw Little Molly standing outside, her hair tied in brilliant yellow ribbons. She still had her doll, Annie, with her. He crouched down to talk to her.

"Uh, hello, Little Molly," Megwadesk said, feeling sad already. Innocence was always used. What did this poor child know? This was terrible, he thought.

"Hello," Little Molly said and smiled. "I know you!"

Mimi stood behind Megwadesk, wondering what this was all about. Little Molly cupped her mouth to hide her missing teeth.

"Who sent you here, Little Molly?" Megwadesk asked. "Who wants this sugar?"

"My grammy. She's not feeling good."

Megwadesk looked up at Mimi and nodded. Then he told Little Molly, "I'm sorry, Little Molly, but we don't have much sugar. We'll run out by tonight."

He returned the empty cup to her.

"My daddy gave you money. I seen him. He wasn't mean to you," Little Molly asked, backing away.

Megwadesk remembered the bills Skoltch had stuffed in the left pocket of his jacket. He took them out and gave them to the girl. There was a desperate eagerness in his trembling hands to get the money away from him. There was no doubt he *had* been deliberately cruel to Skoltch, while Skoltch had, at least, tried to be kind to him. He felt confused. Where did Skoltch really stand? He asked himself, *What's the greater sin, eh, to betray a mother or to allow evil to have its way?*

"I'm not mean," he said. "Here. See? Now I give you money. But I can't give you sugar."

He wanted to explain to her that he wasn't being mean. For a moment he was most anxious to prove his innocence. Then he asked, *But wouldn't it be just 'nother mean act to prove my innocence, eh, 'cause won't that take showing up her grandmother's guilt? No. It's better for me to look bad, to look stingy. Children gotta believe in their grandmothers, eh. Children need to think that things are fair and square in this world, eh, even if fair and square is only in fairy tales.* He almost went so far as to fish out his wallet to give Little Molly more money, but he stopped in time by reminding himself that Mimi did not like to see him give money away.

"I'm sorry. I can't give you anything else. Maybe if your father sent you I could have helped," he said and he bit his lip. He had said too much already. The little girl would wonder now what was so bad about her grandmother in comparison to her father. Already she was frowning.

"Bye, bye," Megwadesk said.

"Bye," Little Molly said. As she turned to walk away, her head bowed and the yellow ribbons flopping, Megwadesk closed the door.

"What was that about?" Mimi asked. "Don't you know that poor girl's grandmother broke her arm last night? I feel bad now that Old Molly and I ever got into it."

"She broke her arm? How'd it happen?"

"My mum said she heard she fell off her bed and crashed to the floor while she was sleeping. But your mum said she heard it happened in the barn. She banged into some bricks because it was too dark for her to see."

"I'll tell you what I think happened," Megwadesk said and he told her about the strange things that had happened to him during the night. Mimi listened with growing horror.

When he was done, she exclaimed, "Nisgam! I wasn't wrong then! And both your mum and my mum agreed that it was her *left* arm she broke, too! No wonder you didn't give that girl any sugar."

Mimi knew that witches could regain power over those they once used to manipulate by winning their sympathies or by soliciting acts of kindness from them.

"If I can help it, eh," Megwadesk said, "her arm'll never heal properly. I'm not giving her an inch."

Mimi nodded. She did not know what to say. There was too much to think about.

"Are you hungry?" she asked him.

Megwadesk walked towards the bedroom.

"I am," he said, "but I'm just too tired to eat right now. I'm gonna sleep a bit. Why don't you join me?"

"Nisgam! What if somebody walks in and sees us sleeping in broad daylight? What will they think? They'll say, 'Those couple are the laziest people I've ever seen!'"

"Come on, sugar. Just lie down with me until I fall asleep. Then you can creep out of bed 'n' go show the whole world what a hard worker you are."

"You look like you'll fall asleep the minute you close your eyes."

"Then you shouldn't have to idle too long, eh."

Mimi shook her head, laughed, and said, "Well, go wash up first, then!"

Mimi took the pot off the stove, set it on the table to cool, and then walked into their small bedroom. Megwadesk took off his shirt. There was a black stain on his bandage. He removed the bandage and the plantain leaves. The puncture had closed. The swelling was down.

After Megwadesk washed himself, standing in a basin of water, stripped but for a towel, he went to join Mimi in the bedroom, who had already stripped and was under the covers. The warm blankets felt good but Mimi's warmer body felt much better.

He snuggled up behind her and wrapped his arms around her waist. He stroked her stomach but he did not feel any noticeable difference in size. Then his hands wandered up to her breasts and he kissed her back between her left shoulder and her neck. His heart bobbed and soaked in a streaming tub of tranquillity. Now that he had money again, he promised to buy her something precious the next time he went to town. He studied the sunlight shining on her dark

145

hair, making some strands gleam red. He heard his father saying, "And the Lord rested on the seventh day!" A gust pressed against the curtains through the slightly open window.

"I knew you weren't happy," Mimi said.

"Huh?"

"When I asked you yesterday if you were happy, you said you were. But I knew you weren't. Are you happy now?"

"Yep. Happy to finally sleep, eh, with you by my side."

Mimi reached behind her and stroked his thigh and answered, "I love you, too."

Megwadesk felt the blood coursing through his exhausted body like the waves on the ocean when there was only a breeze and the waves were great, gently undulating swells. The wind grew stronger outside. Wejúsyn was fanning itself.

He thought about Little Molly, about innocence, about the coming child, about what to teach, about religion, about beliefs, about stories true and false, about his responsibility as a father, about conscience, about free will. Then he thought, *Oh, I'm tired right now, eh, 'n' I have to sleep. I'll look after that stuff 'n' sort it all out later.*

Mimi's hair tickled his face. He closed his eyes. Instantly he saw his net. Yes, he would be hauling in bass from now on. He would be going to Trenton again tomorrow. And he knew nothing he did in his dreams could stop the stones falling from the bridge. He fell asleep to the sound of wind whistling through the window.

PRONUNCIATION GUIDE
FOR MICMAC WORDS

Currently there are three orthographies in use throughout Micmac country for writing Micmac. All three – Metallic, Milliea, and Francis-Smith – are based on the Pacifique writing system. I decided not to use any of the three available orthographies for this book because I was concerned that non-Micmac speaking people, raised in English, would apply English pronunciation rules to these orthographies and end up badly mispronouncing words. For example, the Pacifique spelling for the Two-Horned-Serpent is *Tjipitjgam*, which, for a person familiar only with English spellings, looks impossible to pronounce. Therefore, I tried to spell words using the alphabet – most especially the vowels – as they are voiced in English. Hence, I spell the Two-Horned-Serpent as *Jibichgám*. The following alphabet of twenty-six letters, with the pronunciation guide, summarizes the writing system used in this book. Readers must realize, though, that this orthography is not one of the three unofficially endorsed by various Micmac bands.

a as the *u* in "m*u*d."
á as the *a* in "*fa*ther," (or equivalent to two "**a**"s).
b as in the English *b*.
ch as in the English *ch*, but slightly softer.
d as in the English *d*.
e as the *e* in "f*e*d."
é as the *a* in "rec*a*nt," (or equivalent to two "**e**"s).
g as in the English *g*.
h as in the English *h*.
i as the *i* in "d*i*d."
í as the *ee* in "n*ee*d," (or equivalent to two "**i**"s).
j as the *dg* in "e*dg*e."
k as in the English *k*, but slightly softer.
l as in the English *l*.
m as in the English *m*.
n as in the English *n*.
o as the *o* in "*o*r."
ó as the *oa* in r*oa*r, (or equivalent to two "**o**"s).
p as in the English *p*, but slightly softer.
q a guttural g, as the *ch* in the Celtic word "lo*ch*," but softer.

147

s as in the English *s*.
t as in the English *t*, but slightly softer.
u as the *u* in "p*u*ll."
ú as the *oo* in "p*oo*l," (or equivalent to two "**u**"s).
y as the *i* in "s*i*r." (This short, indistinct vowel sound is fre
quently used to slur consonants together.)
w as the English *w*.

GLOSSARY

In the square brackets the words are divided into syllables, with stressed syllables printed in capitals.

Algimu: [AL-GI-mu] *A* **ginab** *who fought the* **Gwedejk.** *He died twice in his old age.* Literally derives from **Algimued** [Al-GIM-mu-ed], *One-Who-Sends-Orders*, which refers to his role as a commander.

Algumid: [AL-gu-mid] *He is drifting on his boat spearing fish during the day (with the help of sunlight, as opposed to using torches or lanterns to spear at night).*

Amudj: [a-MUDJ] *Yes.* Emphatic.

Amudj dagadu: [a-MUDJ da-GA-du] *Yes, indeed.*

Amudj gadu: [a-MUDJ GA-du] *Yes, indeed!* Assertive.

Ána dóq: [Á-na DÓQ] *Alright then.*

Aqq: *And.*

Awógejid: [a-WÓ-ge-JID] *Spider.*

Bana: [BA-na] *Simply.* As in, "It's simply crazy."

Babkutbalud: [BAB-KUT-ba-lud] *The Keeper of Souls.* He is a giant who has his lodge set up at the end of the Milky Way, where the entrance to the Land of Souls is. He carries a huge war club and will not allow any living being past the entrance.

Bugladymúchk: [bu-gl-A-dym-ÚCHK] *The Little People.*

Bunáne: [bu-NÁ-NE] *A New Year greeting.* From the French for, "Have a Good Year!"

Buowin: [bu-o-WIN] *An evil man who possesses extraordinary powers.* Hence, *a warlock.* The term **buowin** is intended to be the very opposite of **ginab.**

Buowinéskw: [bu-o-WIN-ÉSKW] *An evil woman possessing extraordinary powers.* Hence, *a witch.*

Chigdeg: [CHIG-deg] *It is absolutely tranquil.*

Deúmel: [DEÚ-mel] *Spirit ally.* Also refers to objects that are believed to have the power of one's totem.

Dunél: [dun-ÉL] *The slayer of giants.* Many collectors of legends like to portray **Glúskeb** as the Micmac God, who created the first people, but this is not so. People already existed when the Star Woman (Turtle Woman, in some versions) gave birth to the supernatural twins, **Glúskeb** and **Malsum**. In fact, it was to impress the Micmacs with his extraordinary powers that **Malsum** tore his way out of his mother's womb. **Dunél** is the oldest hero-figure recalled in the legends. He appeared ages before **Glúskeb** did and he slew the giants and the giant animals to make the world a better place for the people. Even in that age, people already existed. But neither is **Dunél** the Micmac God.

Edynaha: [e-dyn-A-HA] An exclamation, equivalent to, *That's it!*

Eíoqa: [EÍ-o-qa] An expression of admonishment, equivalent to, *Don't be foolish!*

Elísasid: [e-LÍ-sa-sid] Literally, *He-Is-Sewed-Up*. It is a spirit that appears to a person when someone close to him or her is on the verge of death. The spirit is a terrifying sight to behold. The only way to save the dying person from death is to embrace the horrible-looking spirit. It is called **elísasid** because in the olden days the Indians used to sew shut the eyes and the mouths of corpses. The spirit, too, has its eyes and mouth sewed up, but the seams burst open as soon as one makes a move to embrace it. This spirit is also known as **amalegynéj** [a-ma-LE-gyn-ÉJ] which means *The-Sheeted-One*. The spirit is usually draped in what looks like a sheet.

Éhe: [É-he] *Yes*. An agreement.

Éq: *Yes!* An emphatic agreement or an emphatic assertion.

Gejidoq: [GE-ji-DOQ] *He knows*.

Gesalul: [GE-sa-lul] *I love you*.

Gesbiaduksi: [GES-bi-a-DUK-si] *I have completed my story*.

Gesbiaduksid: [GES-bi-a-DUK-sid] *He has completed his story*. A traditional expression for ending a story.

Ginab: [gi-NAB] *A benevolent man possessing extraordinary powers*. He can be a warrior, a medicine person, a mystic, a prophet, a statesman, a chief, a hunter, or many other things, but his role is always as a helper to the people and he must have secret knowledge. A woman of such a nature is called **ginabéskw** [gi-nab-ÉSKW].

Gisúlk: [gi-SÚLK] *God, the Creator*.

150

Glu: [gl-U] *A large predatory flying monster.* I have seen this word translated as "condor," and this may be a good secondary definition for the word, because it helps to bring it into modern usage. However, this name originally signified a terrible flying beast (not necessarily a bird) who, in ancient times, preyed on people.

Glúskeb: [GLÚ-skeb] *Supernatural hero of the Micmacs.* Literally, *He-Is-A-Deceptive-Speaker.* He came from a supernatural mother, who descended to earth to give birth to two sons. He was the older of the twins and the just one of the two. Countless stories exist about him. He shaped much of **Mígymági** [MÍ-gym-Á-gi], the Country of the Micmacs, and he did many wonderful things before he left. He promised to return when the Micmacs were most in need of him.

Goqwei: [go-QWEI] *What.* Also means *very*, when used to emphasize a phrase or word.

Gugwesk: [gu-GWESK] *Man-eating giants.* In legends, infant-heroes often battled these monsters, which is a motif that parallels but much more amplifies the David and Goliath theme. In Micmac, the game of tag is called **gugwej** [gu-GWEJ], or "man-eating giant." The one who is "it" is the **gugwej**.

Guís: [gu-ÍS] *You, my son.* An address of affection.

Gwedejk: [GWE-dejk] *Mohawks.* Many scholars believe that the archaic meaning of this name refers to another nation of the Iroquoian family, the St. Lawrence Iroquois, who lived in Hochelaga.

Gwimu: [gwi-MU] *Loon.* One of **Glúskeb's** messengers. He flew messages across bodies of water. Loon is said to have a haunting cry now because he misses **Glúskeb**.

Jenúg: [je-NÚG] *Giants.* Deadly monsters that **Dunél** slew. Also indicates powerful wizards capable of increasing their size. In contemporary usage, some people use the term to indicate the creature more commonly known as sasquatch.

Jibichgám: [ji-BICH-GÁM] *A giant two-horned serpent.* In mythology they played various roles. At times they were benign; other times they were terribly destructive; frequently they were a test a hero had to overcome; and sometimes they represented alien societies. Today the word refers to *crocodile.* It is also a term of insult, and when used that way is regarded as a terribly offensive word.

Jínym or **Jínyma**: [JÍ-nym] *Man.* A term of respect.

Kwéi: [kw-ÉI] *Greetings!* Archaic.

Ligasudi: [li-ga-SU-di] *Shield.* Literally, *The-thing-to-hide-behind.*

Malsum: [MAL-sum] *The villain archetype in Micmac stories.* Literally, **Wolf.** An archaic term. One of the supernatural twins born from Star Woman (or Turtle Woman). His first crime was to kill his mother by springing out of her side. He committed many grievous deeds until **Glúskeb** turned him to stone.

Máli: [MÁ-li] *Mary, mother of Jesus.*

Meda: [ME-da] *Because.*

Megwadesk: [me-gwa-DESK] *Red northern lights.* Literally, *It is flashing (or striking) red.* Another name for the northern lights is **Wegadesk** [weg-a-DESK], which means *Angry-flashes.*

Melkabilasid: [MEL-ka-bil-A-sid] *The war chief who led the Micmacs to victory against the* **Gwedejk***.* Literally, *Tied-In-A-Hard-Knot,* or *Powerfully-Knotted.* He was a **ginab** and, as his power-name indicates, nothing could undo him. In other dialects of Micmac, he is called **Mejilabegádasij** [ME-ji-la-be-GÁ-DA-sij], which means the same thing.

Messkíg: [mess-GÍG] *Large.* An ironic name for a reserve that has had most of its lands illegally taken.

Mégadu: [MÉ-GA-du] An exclamation, equivalent to, *Oh, my God!* Also, when used to modify a word or phrase, it heightens meaning. For example, **Weltdeg** [WELT-deg], by itself means, *It looks nice,* but, **Mégadu weltdeg**, means, *It is beautiful!*

Mimi: [mi-mi] A diminutive for **mimiges** [mi-mi-GES], which means *Butterfly.*

Mígymwesu: [MÍ-gym-we-SU] *A wizard in the woods who lures people to his abode through the entrancing music of his flute.* Literally, *I-Call-The-People-(Micmacs)-With-My-Flute-Music.* It is said he wears a red feather or a red cap, has leaves for his covering, and transforms people into animals.

Mnduágig: [MN-du-Á-gig] *Hell.* Literally, *The-Land-Of-Evil-Spirits.*

Moquá: [mo-QWÁ] *No.*

Na: *There!*

Nabéw: [na-BÉW] *Rooster.*

Nadóq: [na-DÓQ] *Okay!* An affirmative usually used to recapitulate a point or to return to the last point of discussion. It can also be used to indicate agreement.

Nidab: [ni-DAB] *My friend.*

Nisgam: [NIS-gam] *God, the Grandfather.* Also an archaic term of veneration for the sun.

Nisgam gejidoq: [NIS-gam GE-ji-DOQ] *God knows!*

Nisgam nuduid: [NIS-gam NU-du-id] *As God hears me!* Equivalent to "As God is my witness."

Nuduid: [NU-du-id] *He/she hears me.*

Nugú: [nu-GÚ] An expression usually of playful admonishment. (Although it can also be used to express real displeasure.) It is equivalent to, *Quit it!*

Nujísawed: [nu-JÍ-sa-wed] Literally, *The-One-Who-Weaves.*

Oquetédud: [OQ-uet-É-dud] An exclamation expressing joy, usually over an accomplishment. It also expresses great satisfaction over the work of others. It is used to cheer on oneself and others. Equivalent to, *Right on!*

Set-Ból: [SET-ból] *Saint Paul.*

Skoltch: *Frog.*

Wabus: [WA-bus] *Rabbit.* One of **Glúskeb's** messengers. He usually sent messages over land.

Wasoqejid: [wa-so-QE-jid] *Firefly.* Literally, *The-Little-One-Who-Glows.*

Wejúsyn: [WE-JÚ-syn] *A giant bird whose beating wings caused storms.* The word is related to the name for wind, **udjúsyn** [ud-JÚ-syn].

Weladeg: [we-la-DEG] *It glows beautifully.*

Welamul: [we-LA-MUL] *I find you beautiful.*

Wigewigús: [wi-GEW-i-gús] *October.* Literally, *The-Moon-Of-Fattening-Animals.*

Winpi: [WIN-pi] *The wizard of the north, who abducted members of Glúskeb's household to lure Glúskeb to battle.* Literally, *I-Am-Stationed-In-A-Wrong-(Or-Evil)-Manner.*

Ybchilásij: [Yb-CHI-LÁ-sij] *Let (whoever - the man or the woman) sit in the place of honour.* A formal greeting reserved for respected visitors. Although addressed to the second person singular, the request is phrased as though referring to the third person singular.

Ykdánug: [yk-DÁ-nug] *The ocean shore.* In many places where there are breakwaters, the breakwaters become known as **ykdánug**. The ocean side of the breakwaters is called **ásikdánug** [á-SIK-DÁ-nug].